SHORT-STORIES FROM THE PAST, PRESENT, AND FUTURE

FABRICATED REALITIES

SK ALHAM ZAIN

First Published in April 2023

ISBN: 978-93-5741-368-8

BLUEROSE PUBLISHERS

www.BlueRoseONE.com

info@bluerosepublishers.com

+91 8882 898 898

Cover Design:

Sk Alham Zain

Typographic Design:

Rohit

Distributed by: BlueRose, Amazon, Flipkart

This book is dedicated to my parents, Momma and Papa, thank you for all the support and without whom none of it was possible.

Preface

"Fiction is the truth inside a lie."~Stephen King

My fellow fictionoisseurs! (No need to google the term, I made it up). I humbly invite you to a ride in which you would visit alternate universes with characters that you may want to live with or perhaps shove a knife at.

"Fiction", "Fantasy", "Thrill", "Escapism", you would find it all here, aid your mind to imagine, and visualize the realities that I have fabricated. What does the future entail? No one knows for sure. Explore the possibilities of dystopian circumstances in "Tales from the Future".

Travel back in time into the lush medieval lands or the truly treacherous sea in "Tales from the Past".

And if you prefer to stay in contemporary times, "Tales from the Present" has got your back.

I have carefully crafted each story with passion to compile them as my very first book, my first opportunity to tell my stories to the world. I would finally render myself, A Storyteller.

Special Thanks

There are a handful of people I would like to acknowledge who brought this dream into existence.

THANK YOU...

Prof. Soumyajit Chandra, for reviewing and guiding me towards light.

Mrs. Sani Ahmed, for unveiling my passion for literature that lurked in my core.

Ambreen Hossain, on whose shoulder my arm rested when my mind birthed the idea, and being there on every step.

Sharjeel and Zamil Bhai for being my initial readers, and providing me with diverse perspectives.

Contents

Tales from the Future

Fabricated Realities

Tales From the Past

Monarch Trilogy

Dead Knight

Knighthood. A post held with honor, and respect. In the year 1272, a knight named Palmer sat on a high mountain freezing to his bones. All that heavy knight armor was no good in weather conditions this severe, he was a few minutes away from being seriously frostbitten. There was a blizzard that swept through Palmer's broken body. With a greatsword in his right hand and a shield in the other, he knelt with his head looking down at the ground. "Am I defeated?" he whispered to himself, "It cannot be...I am close, I can... I can feel it."

The Knight's journey had been long and tedious. He had gone through various challenges and faced tremendous difficulty to reach this point. He cannot back out now. Neither does he want to. Palmer gazes into the symbol of his clan imprinted on his shield and stands up at once. He continues to walk up the mountain. His legs sank to his knees with every step. His plume was waving like a flag in the unforgiving wind that had the power to blow the strongest of wills away. But not Palmer--- he was determined to reach the peak. The Iron and steel that were molded in the flames of the volcano 'Fehro' were now cold as ice. It wasn't the first time it was cold though, the armor had been in similar conditions before. "The Great Battle of Jarphor"- a fight between the North and South. Palmer fought bravely for the South with his comrades, given the fact they were not accustomed to fighting in cold snowy regions. Palmer was the sole survivor of the battle. The very last warrior. Literally, all others had died except him. He limped his way into the North king's Castle holding a severed head. There was no one to stop him. Even the King's guards had died in the Battle, which allowed him to walk into the castle freely without any resistance. He entered the Great Hall where the king sat on his throne chugging his wine.

"So... you have come to kill me," said the king proudly.

The Blood in Palmer's Plume dripped down making a trail as he walked towards the surrendered king. He threw the decapitated head at his feet. The king looked down to find his son's eyes, stripped of life. The King laughed and kicked the head away from himself. The king didn't stop laughing and Palmer came close. He placed his great sword on the king's shoulder and with one clean strike cut off his head. After removing his body from the throne he placed himself there, sheathed the great sword, and through the gaps in his helmet scanned the hall. That was the story of how Palmer killed his own Father.

Palmer slipped and fell occasionally as he tried to stumble his way to the top of the mountain. He always picked himself up after every fall. His shield and sword support him. "Just a little more."

Palmer had many other names that people called him around the Kingdom. Some he knew of, and some, if he heard them, would send him into a killing spree. Palmer was known for many great things, terrible, but great. Killing his father, going on a rampage and slaughtering hundreds of soldiers in battle, and being the lone survivor in "The Great Battle of Jarphor". Once during a war, he invaded a church along with his fellow warriors. He mercilessly killed the bishop and the worshipers in the church without a second thought. He came across his men rounding up children.

"What are you doing?" Asked Palmer gripping his great sword, "Why are you not killing them?"

"You must be out of your mind Palmer," said a fellow knight, "They are just children."

Through the opening of his helmet, Palmer watched the children, all sobbing. "Alright, I shall take them to our camp, raid the next sector."

Palmer led the children down to where their camp was. "In this cave, hurry up."

All the children went inside but the last one; he was the eldest of them all. "Sire, where is the camp?"

Palmer moved his head towards him, his red plume rippling. "The camp is right at the tip of my sword," he said before thrusting the blade into the child's throat. Later the other knights found eleven bodies in that cave.

All children. It was a massacre that gave Palmer the title "The Slayer of the Innocent."

The blizzard, stronger than ever, pushed Palmer to his knees repeatedly, but he was almost there. Still equipped with every piece of armor that he had, with his loyal sword and trusty shield, he treads forward.

When Palmer was young, he aspired to be a great knight. For fifteen years, he trained and became one. The first seven years were decent; he won minor wars and defended his country against invasions. During his first major war, he and his company had chased a group of adversaries into an unknown cavern that kept on going deeper. It was unexplored and the decision of entering a strange uncharted cavern is never a good idea. Palmer and his company were stuck in there for days unable to find a way out. One by one, they started to die until Palmer was the only one remaining. On the verge of death, he saw something, a vision of Eris, believed to be the evilest of the Greek pantheon.

"One who lies here alone, what do you seek?"

Palmer's lips barely moving utters "Life."

"I shall grant you a hundred years, only if one promises to be one of mine, to do what I shall say, to do what I ask, to do everything my heart desires."

Palmer at the edge of slipping into the afterlife mumbles, "I give you... my word."

Palmer was then seen walking out of the cavern, with pride and a flaming plume on his helmet. No one saw him remove his helmet ever since. With an extraordinary sword by his side and his chest high, he resembled a demigod.

"The peak...I see it," said Palmer.

"He is there, Hermes stands there," whispered Eris.

Palmer hobbled his way to the top of the mountain where the silhouette of a figure appeared.

"Hermes!" screamed Palmer with all the remaining strength he had left. "I shall have you at the end of my blade."

"You shall not," said the silhouetted figure, "Also you are too far gone for me to save you."

"I need no savior, I have already been saved."

"Oh Eris, you did find a worthy puppet, but still... not strong enough."

Palmer was about to stab the figure, but in quick succession Hermes turned and with just a simple flick of his fingers sent his helmet flying, exposing Palmer's face with veins that ran all over his face, eyes blackened around, no hair and a half jaw missing. It was the face of a man who has been dead a long time.

"I pity you," said Hermes softly before backing off and disappearing into the snowstorm.

Palmer's body collapsed and his head spasmed. The blade of the great sword turned into ash and Eris appeared before him. She looked down on him with disgust yet a face of gratification. She uttered "Amusing" before vanishing into the blizzard. A drop of blood exited Palmer's lifeless eyes and trickled down to the snow. "*A hundred years...*"

~God's Amusement

King

Nobility. It does not come from fighting wars tirelessly for the country. The person is born royal. Blue blood runs in their veins. Percy, the son of the great king of the North marched down the hall. The Castle walls vibrated as soldiers, with shields, swords and banners followed Percy. They were heading to war, a war if lost would prove fatal for the Northern kingdom. Percy held his father's great sword, 'The Lionheart', a name received after the king had slain a pride of lions, which attacked him on his hunt. The sword was passed down to Percy, who honored the blade.

Percy exited the castle with the strong men behind him. He turned to look at his father who stood at a high place with a look of pride. He displayed no emotion for his son going to, war: he was old and did not have the same spirit as he did before.

The Northern king, James, when young, was a quick and agile warrior. His ability to swing a sword was unmatched in all the kingdoms. The speed with which he fought was a remarkable sight. Swift and precise slashes and in no time his enemies would go down. He went to faraway lands to find adventure, which he did. He fought many animals and creatures but the major one of them all was a Dragon. In the distant lands of 'Rilada', flew a majestic creature, one of the last of its kind. The flying beast was named 'Tyror' by the local farmers and storytellers. James after hearing horrifying tales of the dragon decided to take matters into his own hands and slay the great beast. His father, Edward, the king at the time, did not allow him to go on such a reckless adventure. He argued it was stupid and vile. James was Edward's only son, the only heir to the throne, and he could not afford to lose him. The elderly King Edward begged James not to leave and even restrained him from doing so, but the heart of James was burning with passion. He persuaded guards and with the help of his warrior friends, he snuck out one night.

He traveled for days before reaching Rilada. Naturally, there was no one there, just ruins of a town that once existed, now scorched by flame. Far on the horizon James saw a mountain, and right on top the figure of the flying beast.

"Is that…him? questioned James, "That's Tyror, is it not?"

"It seems so my lord," said Edel, one of his warrior friends, "We better prepare before we fight."

The group arranged their weapons and got ready for the major hunt. There was not a trace of fear on James' face which helped his group to maintain high energy and morale. In leadership, confidence is key and James had plenty.

'Tyror' soared into the sky not knowing that these men were there to kill him. The group slept in a cave near the ruins of Rilada. The sun rose and with it, raised the men with intentions to slay the dragon. A few hours after dawn, they collected their weapons and moved out. They flared torches to attract the attention of the flying beast and they did. Down came Tyror growling at the men.

"Fire at will" screamed James and a volley of arrows shot at the dragon.

The arrows penetrated Tyror's skin and he screamed in pain. Fire brewed inside its mouth and eventually, it rained down. James and his company were able to run out of harm's way and continue firing. James threw a bunch of spears at the dragon and thanks to his high precision; it stabbed the dragon right in its eyes. The dragon was blinded and blew fire in all directions. James' company wasn't that lucky. Bodies fell. Burned and being stepped on by the dragon all of them died except Edel and James, himself. Tyror tried to fly but James sprinted towards him with abnormal speed, jumped high, and with one clean slash of his blade tore the dragon's wings. It lost balance and fell to the ground.

"What? How did he?" whispered Edel to himself. He was shocked after watching James perform with succession.

The dragon growled and got back on his feet.

"Watch out, my lord!" shouted Edel.

Tyror sensed which direction the noise had come from and shot a fireball at him. Edel witnessed the fireball approaching his broken body and with no intentions or power to move out of the way, he accepted his fate. Until he felt a tackle. He was saved. James had saved him.

Edel looked at James with disbelief and thought 'He was so far away from me...'

James stood up and noticed the blind dragon charging in their direction. He unsheathed his sword once more and rushed it head-on. James slid below Tyror, stabbed its neck and sliced it all the way to its tail. The blood and organs of the dragon plopped out and the pace of the galloping dragon slowed down. Edel saw the dragon coming towards him, slowing down. The dragon's head dropped on Edel's shivering body and the sharp end of the dragon's chin impaled him. James walked around its body to check on Edel to find him dead.

"Ah, a real shame," said James out loud, "I saved this fool once; I can't always do that, can I?"

James looked at the dragon's body and found Hermes sitting on top with his fist on his chin.

"Well well well. I suppose not" uttered Hermes "But I have saved you multiple times."

"I was rolling down the mountain, yes, it was one hell of a perilous mountain, but you only caught me because you were passing by."

"Don't be ungrateful now, there was an avalanche too."

"I am just messing with you, Hermes. You know I am eternally grateful."

"I saw good in you James, that is why I have lent you some of my powers. It is temporary. Enjoy it while you can."

"You don't have to remind me of that."

James, satisfied with the thrill of this adventure then wandered off into a neighboring kingdom of "Vaelow" where he was welcomed auspiciously. This kingdom fell under the northern terrain and hence under the king. James spent a few months celebrating and drinking his heart content. It was here he fell in love with Princess Briana and decided to marry her. The couple then traveled back to Edward's castle and upon their arrival, the news was broken to him that his father Edward had passed away. On one hand, he felt immense sadness and the urge to cry on the other his heart rejoiced, he was the king now.

In the years that followed Briana gave birth to a beautiful daughter and two sons. The daughter was the eldest but she abandoned the kingdom at the age of twenty and ran away. No one knew the reason but they assumed that she was tortured by James. The two sons, who were twins, were named Percy and Palmer. Percy was always the favorite one. He was well-mannered, housed etiquettes, was fluent to speak to the people, had unbelievable skill, a sharp brain, and to top it all, he was a fine swordsman. Palmer felt lonely. He was bested by his own brother in everything they did. Frustration built up and with a desire to defeat his brother in anything, he began his journey to become a knight. A knight he would become not for the North but the South. Like his sister, he abandoned the north kingdom and pledged his life to the south. He trained extensively. He poured his blood and sweat into it. He became a knight, an excellent one, he earned titles, and he became...a demigod. He earned malicious titles after... one of them being "The Slayer of the Innocent."

James' eyes flashed with the image of his two sons Palmer and Percy playing around the hall with wooden swords as he gazed down on Percy marching towards war. "The Great Battle of Jarphor." He was going to fight his own brother.

The two armies stood by on the battlefields staring at each other, waiting for their commander to say the word. Percy treads forward to negotiate a deal with the South but as soon as Palmer notices Percy approaches he orders his men to charge.

"No honor eh!" says Percy, "For King James!"

The Battle goes on. Men fought, they bludgeoned each other until either of them fell. Palmer and Percy slaughtered many men. Palmer impaled the gut of the last Northern soldier before looking up to spot his brother. Percy is doing the same thing but a hundred meters away from him. All are dead, except for the two brothers. Corpses lay everywhere, it was impossible to spot a dry patch of land among all the bloodshed of people from both sides. The snow on the ground was soaked and appeared scarlet. The two brothers walked quickly toward each other and eventually they collided. The cling of their blades striking together could be heard at 'Fehro'. The brothers engage in a brilliant sword fight, slashing armor, parrying blows, and occasionally pushing each other away to make space. The red flaming plume on Palmer's helmet ripples as he tries to thrust his blade. The metal of their armor made noise, they stepped on the bodies, arms, and legs of their fallen men, but they did not stop dueling. Percy fought with immense concentration until he saw a figure float behind Palmer. A woman with wings and on one hand a double-sided shortsword. He lost his focus for a moment, which gave Palmer the opening for a strong strike that broke 'Lionheart' in half. Palmer pushed Percy; he fell back and looked up to see Palmer point his great sword at him. Percy was defeated.

"I won, brother!" sighed Palmer, "I finally won!"

Percy squinted his eyes a little and gawked at the gaps in Palmer's helmet.

"I knew my brother. Palmer. A person with flair to prove himself. But you...You are not him...You are not my brother...I don't see him...he has been dead a long time..."

Eris appeared behind Palmer. He lifted his great sword and severed Percy's head.

Palmer marched up King James' castle.

"Hermes, help me," said James aloud sitting on his throne, "I know you have been gone a long time, but I need you now. I have a bad feeling..."

James coughed as he chugged a glass of wine. The doors of the throne room opened wide and in came Palmer with Percy's severed head. Eris levitated behind Palmer, as he grew closer to James.

'Eris...' thought James, laughing before his head got sliced by Palmer.

~Where are the Gods when you need them?

Queen

"...I told her that she can drown a thousand times and I wouldn't care", said a bearded man chugging his ale from a wooden goblet, "I have used her enough, I am exhausted, I want someone new, she is a pain in my bottom now."

A group of ax-wielding savages sat on the tables of the 'Velton Inn', discussing their lives, Breaking the benches, and drinking unsupervised. It was four o'clock in the morning and the end of their drinking was nowhere near the horizon.

"Bring us another Barrel!" exclaimed Barom, the leader of the group.

The innkeeper was a simple man and wanted no trouble, but there was a limit to everything and these savages were way past it.

"Sire, do you mind not jumping on the benches?" asked the innkeeper politely, "You have broken four of them already."

Barom's gaze shifted to the innkeeper and he stood up at once. He approached the innkeeper with his eyes fixed on his; he grabbed him by his neck and held him in the air. The innkeeper's legs dangling, trying to reach the ground, held Barom's hand in desperation.

"How dare you speak to me that way, peasant!?" He said choking the innkeeper, "Don't you know who we are?"

The innkeeper struggled and tried to speak, but still had no guts to hit Barom or even push him away. He knew, if he tried to hurt Barom in any way, even in self-defense, he would be either tormented for life or killed.

"We are the Vilx, and you do not mess with us. We are fearless, brave, wild, yet-

"Disciplined, compassionate, and sharp..." a voice interrupted, "Isn't that right? Barom...?"

Barom lost the look of Pride and adopted the face of rage. He turned to find an individual in a cloak with a hood sitting at the very corner of the inn, eating berries. Barom lets go of the innkeeper's neck, he falls and coughs. His steps now close in on the mysterious figure.

"So you know a lot about us, don't you?" Barom said softly, and then increased his voice to shout, "That gives you no right to speak when I am talking!"

His comrade passed him an ax. He clutched the handle of the ax firmly as he approached the hooded figure, still munching on berries. Barom sat right beside the individual and put his hand around the person's shoulder. His goons followed his lead and all of them sat or stood surrounding the table. "Were you saying something child?" uttered Barom noticing a smaller body structure than he expected.

"Yes", said a feminine voice, "The Vilx call themselves brave and fearless, but they were the first ones to flee when 'Rilada' was falling. One look at the dragon and with a snap of a finger, the Vilx packed their gear and fled."

Barom, enraged, slammed the table with his fist from which he held the ax, knocking the berries to the floor, and said, "You talk foul of our fore-fathers? Oh, you have some nerve!"

Barom's goons started to crack their knuckles as if they were getting ready to punch. Barom blew air at the edge of the ax and said, "I am going to like this...but you girl... will not."

Barom peeked under the cloak to identify a smirk on her white scarred face. He raised his ax and struck it on her leg. Barom felt the ax wedge on her thigh, with a crackling noise, which he thought was her bone. She did not budge, no reaction, no movement. Barom frowned, perplexed. He looked down, his eyes widened and his mustache moved as he exhaled heavily. The ax phased through her thigh and was wedged on the bench they sat on.

She pounced high up in the air, almost touching the ceiling, her cloak waving and rippling as if there was a storm. She landed before them and whipped her cloak away exposing her.

The Vilx bowed down at the sight of her. Before them, stood Eleanor, the 'The Runaway princess' of the northern King.

"Your highness...I..." Barom kneeling, looking at the ground, tried to speak but had no words.

"Your highness?" she inquired, "Oh no Barom. I am not that... well not anymore."

"I have been blessed by the god that you stand before me, your highness," he said without looking at her, "The last time I saw you, you were fleeing from the kingdom after King James ordered to kill you."

"I visited my father a few years after my 'runaway'. He wasn't happy to see me, hence he ordered you to bring my head if I don't leave." She said recollecting her memories, "That was years ago, things must have changed since then right? Or am I delusional?"

"Things have changed, yes your highness, but for the worse," Barom said hesitantly.

"Apart from constant conflict, what else has gone wrong?" she questioned.

"That 'constant conflict' has heated up, it's red hot, your highness..." Barom slowly raised his head, looking at her, "There is a war coming...And it's no ordinary war...it's 'The Great Battle of Jarphor', the snowy regions of Jarphor are going to be soaked in the blood of men. Friend and foe. After all, it is the collision between two brothers. A demigod and the son of the Kingdom. Palmer and Percy..."

A current passed through Eleanor's body and she was left stunned. It was a mountain of information for her to absorb. She was oblivious to the contemporary situation and was stabbed with terror and concern.

"Father..." she whispered under her breath.

"King James still lives. The northern wall has kept its enemies at bay for hundreds of years, but I am afraid under the leadership of Palmer, he has surpassed every one of the other adversaries that we have ever had. His army grows stronger every day and he would strike the hammer onto the heated iron as soon as possible."

"I have to get father out of there", she said with visible concern on her face.

"Do you really want to do that, your highness?" he questioned, "After what happened last time?"

"Mind your own damn business Barom" her cloak rippled as she moved away from him and grabbed the door handle, "I'm sure things would be different this time"

Time passed, the war grew closer and before Eleanor knew it, the day of battle arrived. After days of research, sneaking around, and using her tactical mind, she could sneak inside the castle walls. She hid among the haystacks that were being transported by a farmer into the castle. The farmer's justification for delivering these goods at this fatal moment was, "Let me earn some money before everything goes to hell."

On her way in, she peeked outside, and glimpsed a sight of her brother, Percy, 'The Son of the Kingdom' marching out to war. "Can't even hold his sword properly, yet the best swordsman of his time...baffling", she thought to herself.

After a few minutes, the cart was parked in the stables. She jumped out as the farmer announced that the way was clear. She chucked a pouch full of silver at the man, "Many thanks" she said before disappearing into the castle.

She hustled her way towards the great hall where she was sure her father would sit, hoping for his son Percy's triumphant return. Just before she reached the great hall, the king's guard greeted her. According to the reports, they were also supposed to be in the battle, but they stood before her, the hilts of swords and shields in hand. All four of them frowned at the sight of Eleanor. They had strict orders to kill any intruder and she was no more than one herself. They unsheathed their swords all at once and charged at her.

"I didn't want to do this…"

The first one swung his sword horizontally aiming at her gut. She held her breath and let the blade phase through her body.

"What?" chanted the perplexed guard.

She dropped her cloak and revealed a bow and quiver strapped to her back. She did a backflip over the guard who swung his sword and placed herself looking at all four guards in front. Thanks to her sleight of hands, she took out an arrow from the quiver, pulled the bowstring, and released it to result in a fatal blow directly at the guard's throat. He fell. The remaining three halted for a moment before charging at her once again.

She slid past the second guard swinging the sword and stabbed the back of his knee with an arrow. The third guard tried to stab her with his blade but it proved insignificant as it phased through her stomach. She smacked the third with her bow, leaving him disoriented. The fourth stood there clenching his sword along with his teeth, unable to comprehend the scene before him. Eleanor aimed and shot a powerful arrow at the fourth guard's head. It pierced his helmet with ease. Moreover, in fact, it completely emerged from the other way around. The second guard, with an arrow in his knees, limped towards her to try and strike her. He failed terribly as she buried an arrow deep in the left side of his throat. The third guard remained on the ground trying to pick himself up. She jumped up high and landed on his stomach. He groaned and saw Eleanor in her eyes before she shot an arrow straight into his heart.

She put her cloak back on and opened the grand gates of the great hall and as expected her father, James sat on his throne with a goblet of wine in his hands.

"Disappointment..." he uttered, "I thought my son had returned from the war."

"Father! You have to come with me" she said hurriedly, "It is not safe here for you. I don't want you to die!"

"And why should I listen to the thing that killed my wife?" he took a sip from the goblet, "Do you have an answer to that Eleanor?"

Eleanor's expression turned into rage from concern.

"It was an accident!" she screamed, "How many times are you going to agonize me with that fact!? I loved my mother, more than any of her sons did! Explains why either of them didn't even shed a tear at the funeral."

"It wasn't just you, was it Eleanor? She was there too...the one who gave you the murder weapon. That wrenched bow and arrow!"

"I know it was my fault, it was MY mistake!" her voice cracked, "That was the time I needed you the most! And what did you do? Pushed me away! You banished me! I know...I cannot redeem myself...but give me a chance. My brothers are at war! Even worse, the war against each other! I might lose a brother today, maybe both! Don't make me lose you, father..."

"You lost me when you fired that arrow that killed Briana," he said softly, "I disowned you that very day. You mean nothing to me Eleanor. Now get your impure presence out of here...I am waiting for my son to return."

Eleanor stood there motionless teary eyed filled with fury. She realized she had lost her father and there was no room for redemption. She steps out of the huge, grand gates of the hall and turns back to close them. She sees her father as the gap closed in. With tears overflowing her sore eyes, she grasped a picture of her father staring directly at her with a merciless gaze. She walked down the corridors and at the very end spotted a figure approaching carrying something in his hand. She was collapsing on the inside and nothing mattered. The two walked and brushed shoulders with each other. It was then she noticed the severed head of Percy held by his hair.

"Palmer? Is that you?" she said without turning to look at him.

"Palmer...a name I haven't heard in a long time...long time" he laughed maniacally, "Alas, he is dead...been dead a long time..."

He continued to walk. She did the same.

She distracted herself from the fact that she had lost her family by hunting, drinking, and other miscellaneous tasks. She vanished from the radar and lived in a cave many kilometers away from the kingdom.

She sat by the fire just staring at it, letting her thoughts cluster in her brain and forcing her eyes to shed tears.

"You know it wasn't your fault", said a mysterious female voice, "If it was someone's fault, then it was mine."

"A goddess accepting a mistake that wasn't her," she said without moving a muscle, "You are one of the good ones."

"We are not all bad," she said quietly.

"Why did you give me that bow and quiver that day?" she whimpered lightly, "I was just a child..."

There was a moment of silence until it broke as the mysterious figure spoke again.

"I bring news."

Eleanor turned to her. "What news can you give me...Artemis?"

The people of your Kingdom are suffering, famine, lack of resources, it is in flames. People are dying for various reasons, sickness, riots, and revolts, and they are even taking their own lives. Your brother Palmer is an abysmal king. It is a shame to even call him king.

"What am I supposed to do?" she questioned, "It's not my business."

"Hermes is back and he promised your father something. He promised that if after his demise, the kingdom falls apart, he is going to take necessary steps to restore the glory of the kingdom" Artemis levitated around Eleanor.

"So what is Hermes going to do?" Eleanor's eyes widened.

"It seems Palmer is possessed by Eris, an evil goddess, and Hermes's rival."

"Is he going to kill Palmer?" interrogated Eleanor.

"Palmer is already dead Eleanor...and it has been a long time since that has happened. The person you saw that day...wasn't him" Artemis places her tender arms on her shoulder, "Trust me, we climb the mountain tomorrow, to see the Dead Knight fall."

Eleanor obliged and that is what they did. Eris, lured by Hermes, guided Palmer to the peak of the mountain. Hermes ended up killing the vessel of Palmer before feeling immense remorse. However, the deed was done. It was necessary for the greater good of the hundreds of people in the kingdom."

Eleanor, from behind a rock, witnessed the whole scene. She saw Eris utter, "Amusing" before disappearing into the blizzard. She stood beside Palmer's lifeless body gazing and reminiscing the times when he cried on her shoulder after being outperformed by Percy in everything.

Nonetheless, she carried the hilt of Palmer's great sword as the blade turned into ash, and helmet back to the Northern Kingdom. The people gawked in awe, perplexed yet somewhat relieved. They noticed the great sword and the helmet and immediately recognized to whom it belonged, "The Slayer of the Innocent." She did not have to gather the people of the kingdom. They followed her as she walked through the streets. She climbed the stairs of the castle, turned, and looked down on all the people of the kingdom. They knew who stood above them. The daughter of King James.

"The King is dead! I am Eleanor! Daughter of King James. The 'Runaway Princess', Well; now I have returned...and you will call me...your Queen!

~A Tragic Heroine

End of Monarch trilogy

Mind of your Friend

The mind of a human being is a mysterious place. The engine runs all the time, even while asleep. How do we not tire ourselves from thinking all the time? Can't the noise stop for a while? Can the brain shut itself off for just a little bit? Ease us from the pain and chaos that reside and conquer our heads, at least maybe when we sleep. A voice that speaks to us in a low, sometimes grim manner, suggests thoughts that would never pop into a civilized person's mind. Jump from the fifteenth floor, dunk a cold bucket of water over your head, deck a person across the face, stomp a cat to death, or even, strangle a person, torture, murder, or burn them alive... makes me positive that the mind can be a dark place.

Why is this...woman so annoying? Doesn't she have places to be? Instead, she decides to hinder my schedule, which is packed with productive things to do. Is it a curse to look better than an average person? Is being called 'handsome', 'good-looking', 'sharp', and 'attractive' accolades that I must flaunt and be proud of? Is that what it has come to? If that is how it is then my dignity should have been over the roof, after all, over the years I have received many such 'accolades'. This fine woman was adding one more to my list. A conversation to which she was the master and I merely didn't care. Her mouth was moving, and I saw her lips change shapes, they were pink, and lots of blood circulated through them. I guess,I don't know, anatomy was not my strong suit, at least not yet. The locks of hair she played with, twisting them furiously with her index finger, her heart probably pounding, desperate to find love or perhaps a hook-up. The basic needs of a typical woman are made marvelously easy nowadays and continue to dwindle down this road. I wonder where we would stand twenty years from now; they would sleep all around in 2014.

She popped her chest and kept modifying her stance to lure me with her unattractive hesitant charisma. She brought out no reaction from me, I was like a Queen's guard standing on his post. I made it coherently clear that I wanted no part of what she was offering. To cover her shame and embarrassment, she tried to sway away from the conversation to small talk before walking away. Why don't they get it? Just go! Blanketing her shame, saving herself from ignominy. I refuse to shield myself from these social constructs. I do not care what they think of me, validation and approval are what dogs beg for. Who's a good boy? Well, guess what? No one gives a damn!

Thank the devil she did walk off. She stopped, uttered, "I am sorry", and strolled away, her voice fading, she said, "Stupid, so stupid of me..."

Am I sometimes too cruel to them? Should I at least speak when they try to initiate something? No? I enjoy ogling at them, watching their lips, red, brown, pink, black, glittered, glossy; the variety was limitless. Blood, so much blood must flow through their lips to make them appear fresh, plump, and straight gorgeous. Do I want to kiss them? Not necessarily. I am not a lust-filled person looking for any chance that I might get. I would not even like to capitalize on an opportunity presented to me with a silver spoon. I am a decent man; I do consider myself a gentleman. I am a lover...a true one I swear, I want to earn their love, and I wish the same for the other. Once given a proper chance I would prove to them how worthy I could be. However, at the end of the day, its night, yes, but also lies the fact that I absolutely do not care about worldly treasures. I am spiritually pure and that is the primary root of my happiness and carefree nature. I am proud.

The ability to alter someone's mood can be considered a superpower. But to make them do things they don't want to do is the ultimate power one can possess. Won't it be cool if I was able to make someone commit a crime, perhaps a murder? A genuinely awful crime one can commit, but making someone else do it doesn't seem bad at all. My mind cannot possibly fathom the possibility and scenario of my hands stripping away the life of a person. I wonder how my aunt's neighbor did it. The 'Milwaukee Cannibal'. The fascination for me lay in the killing part, although the world cared more about him eating his victims. Jeffry Dahmer was a gentleman, the horrific crimes that he committed were beyond the comprehension of my clustered mind. Taking a life is a humongous sin, and I wish the victim's fate to no one. These people, truly disgust me, Ed Gein did the same thing in the 50s, snatching the lives of a few fellow humans. The fascination for the world stayed away from the murder and went straight to the part where he used their bones as decorations in his bedroom.

I was enraged to hear about Ted Bundy when he confessed to slaughtering thirty young women. I mean, how can you? Another gentleman from the outside with a ghastly interior. What goes inside the minds of these cold-blooded killers? Do they put themselves in the shoes of the other? Do you feel what the victims feel? No. Does the hair on their arm rise with pleasure while gutting the victims? Perhaps.

Another baffling news that greeted my ears a few years back was the tale of John Wayne Gacy, "The Killer clown". My blood pressure increased so much that I had to force myself to laugh. A simple trick to control the pressure. That fat man! I wanted to kill him myself! But then again...I was not him...I am no killer. At least my mind is cleaner than theirs and I hope it persists.

I feel lonely sometimes and wonder why no one has connected with me yet. Trust me! I am a great guy. I can be the best friend that you have. The closest friend with whom you share all your secrets, and yes! I will keep them between us. Somehow, all my friends end up running away. A few of them did scurry off when I confessed my secrets to them. Why can't they be like me? Am I the one leaking their deepest and darkest secrets? No, it's them. Anyway, I have learned my lesson and now no one runs away from me, they cannot, and I will not let them. Oh...no no no they shouldn't run from me. My basement, it's not a bad place, it's dark and gloomy, yes, but I have installed a new high-powered bulb down there so it's not as bad as it previously was. Although the stains on the walls and ground are much more visible, it doesn't bother me. The light has also illuminated my collection on the wall. My most prized possession. Oh, how much of my life I have spent growing the collection. Forty-one pairs of human lips. All different from each other, and I believe that I am just a few more away from getting all the shades that I like. Gazing at them every night gives me an insane dosage of dopamine that my brain truly requires. That's how I survive. A mysterious place, the human mind is. Uncanny, yet brilliant.

~Perspective

Seasick

The Ocean is a majestic place. That's what I thought before boarding my Captain's ship in the year of our Lord 1378. My father had sailed with Captain Vex for years and had grown quite attached to his master. He was thrilled that his son would join this great seafarer. After all, the great Captain Vex was widely known for his adventures; he claims to have owned a massive fleet once, which was "all lost" in the battle against Neptune. He swears that he had defeated the god of the sea and now, the waters are safe for travel and exploration.

I was very excited to be a part of Captain Vex's crew. I got in, thanks to the sweet corrupt system called nepotism. My father, Jonah, was a favourite of Captain Vex's, which is a huge deal. According to my father, he had saved the Captain's life many times, and naturally, this had put him above the rest of the crew. Captain Vex was a noble man; he wasn't an ordinary pirate- he was an honourable commander and crowd-pleaser. He always had his chest high and carried a cane. A duelling cane. He was a skilled warrior, or at least that's what everybody thought...

"Finn, my boy!", exclaimed Jonah, a tall black man, in an accent that was rare on the shores of Europe. "This is the proudest moment of my life! My son, my own flesh and blood, joining his old man to serve the greatest Pirate ever to sail these waters!"

"Yes, Papa, I am grateful," I said, bending down, "Where is Captain Vex?"

"There he is my boy," he said pointing a finger towards the deck, "There he stands tall, watching over us."

I walked toward him and bowed to pay my respect. "Sire, Finn is my name. Son of Jonah."

"Oh, welcome aboard Francesca, lad. I hope you offer the same worth your father did all these years," said Captain Vex. Now he roared, raising his voice, "Come on now! Help those men unload the cargo, get some rest, and we shall set sail first thing at dawn."

I followed his instructions. My eyes opened a few minutes before dawn. I hadn't expected to have slept this well; I had expected that due to the excitement of my first adventure, I wouldn't be able to get sound sleep. But I was wrong. I had slept like a log. It was the last time I would get proper sleep. Chaos followed: I walked around the Francesca, examining the beauty of the enchanting vessel, imagining the reckless and riveting experiences the ship had been part of. My thoughts were interrupted by a strange noise that swelled from the Captain's Chamber. I looked around me to find no one and proceeded to investigate the source of this absurd noise. I climbed the ship and approached the sound. The beautifully crafted wooden doors of Captain Vex's cabin were the only thing that stood between me and the noise. I placed the palm of my hand on the door and just when I was about to push it open, a hand pressed on my mouth. The disembodied hand pulled back, suppressing my mouth from making a sound, and we fell back. Just when my heart was pounding out of my chest and my head filling up with dread, the person whispered, "Calm down son... calm down. It's me, your father...it's Jonah..."

My muscles relaxed, and my fist loosened as his words brought me relief.

"Son, you have to trust me, we need to get out of here, I will explain everythi—"

Suddenly, the cabin door opened and out came a fully uniformed Captain Vex with a smirk on his face, which vanished as soon as he saw us lying down outside his door.

"Jonah... did he see...?"

"He saw nothing, Sire," Jonah answered.

"Get him away from my face!"

My father pulled me away as we scrambled to our feet, "Come Finn, busy day today."

"Another thing!" shouted Captain Vex, "Tell him to stay at home!"

He flung his cape and was on his way to the ship wheel.

"What?" I looked at my father, "How can he... I didn't do anything!"

"I am sorry son, this is it - you cannot sail with us."

"Papa, this has been my dream - all I have ever hoped for!"

"I am sorry, my child," he said with receding steps.

But I was not to be discouraged. Here I am now, hiding among the barrels of rum and fruit. I am not giving up on my dreams so easily. All I want is a chance to redeem myself in the eyes of Captain Vex. My chance came when a storm struck and the Francesca was in potential danger of sinking. I revealed myself to the crew by providing a helping hand. It was useless. I had no experience and due to my lack of knowledge, I pulled some ropes which almost got the ship wrecked onto a small island.

My father saw me from a distance and fell to his knees, bursting out into tears and crying uncontrollably. Deacon, another crew member who knew who I was, briefed the crew about the situation and consoled my father.

"Don't worry, Jonah," said Deacon, sliding his hand around Jonah's back, "We will save him."

Captain Vex was still steering the ship out of the storm, and once it was safe, he sallied forth. With the duelling cane firmly in his hand, he charged toward me.

"Sire! Sire! He saved us!" Screamed Deacon, "We would have all drowned if it wasn't for him!"

Captain Vex's steps halted right before he reached me. "Is that so?"

"Yes, Sire!"

"Are you absolutely certain?"

"Yes, I swear on my mother."

"Deacon...swear on me."

Deacon blinked slowly before uttering, "I swear... on you... Sire."

"Good," said Vex before turning and leaving for his cabin.

Spending time in the vessel had made me seasick and all the glorious stories I was told as a child seemed to be nonsensical. This was no tale of a brave and strong pirate. It was one of those cautionary tales that proclaim "All that glitters is not gold". The more time passed, the more Captain Vex appeared cruel. He lost his temper during minor inconveniences and even threatened to kill his crew members. I did not foresee this.

Time passed.

"Bring him!"

I was woken up by the screaming and chaos. I opened my eyes to find out I had passed out on the deck for lack of sleep. I saw my father drag a crewmate, holding his hair and throwing him to the ground.

"Walk the plank!" shouted Captain Vex. "I didn't see anything, my lord! Forgive me! Let me go!" begged the condemned man.

"I SAID, WALK THE DAMN PLANK!"

I then saw my father pull the crewmate's hair and push him towards the plank.

"Do it!"

The broken man crawled his way to the brink of the plank. He turned, on his knees. "My lord, please ..."

Captain Vex pulled out a flintlock from his right holster and shot the man in his head. The body recoiled, fell, and splashed into the vast ocean.

"Stay away from my cabin," he said softly but loud enough for me to hear. "Do you peasants hear me?! STAY. AWAY. FROM. MY. CABIN!"

"Yes, Captain!" all of the crew chanted together.

My curiosity grew, but it wasn't enough to risk my life to investigate. I was patient. I was least interested in what lay beyond the Captain's cabin door.

The cabin doors...were beautifully crafted. The woodwork on the door was fascinating. From the top, a sea horse ejects water from his mouth, spraying it onto a pod of dancing dolphins. It looked like the seahorse was flying above the ocean, showering on the dolphins. Beneath the dolphins, bubbles rise from a school of fish swimming away from an angler fish. Is it chasing them? Maybe... and below all of that, a pair of eyes were peeking through a trident.

"Finn," said Deacon, "What do you think you are doing?"

I look behind me to see Deacon wrapped in a blanket.

"What? Are you alright, Master Dee?"

"Don't worry about me child, remove your hand from there..."

"My hand...?" I snap out, my eyes open to the fullest and I spot my hand clutching the handle of the Captain's Cabin door. I let go of it and back off. "Master Deacon, I swear, I didn't know."

Deacon coughed violently before falling to his knees. He muttered gruffly, "There is a storm brewing. We better be vigilant."

He was correct. An hour later, the winds started to run wild and the waves became treacherous. The Captain held the wheel and the crew struggled to keep the ship from sinking. I was young and almost always seasick; my body still hadn't adapted to the sailor's life. I often did what I was asked to do but they didn't trust me. They gave me minor tasks or even mock tasks, like pulling a rope that affected nothing. I wasn't complaining though. This storm was brutal. It ragdolled my skinny body and tossed me all over the vessel until it hurled me right at Captain Vex's cabin door.

"I am not going in... I am... not..." I screamed, as my eyes scanned the door and fixed it on the door handle. "Just... a peek maybe... "

I brushed my hands past the wooden carpentry and onto the handle. I pushed open the door, poking my head inside. It was dark, but in the distance, I saw a blue crystalline glow. I slid inside, and advanced towards the source of the bizarre light. I rubbed my eyes to see clearly, and reaching the glowing entity, I found a glass container, and in it, water. A shark, the size of a couple of rum barrels was floating on the surface. I touched the lifeless shark - it turned to reveal human limbs attached to its belly - near the fins. I recoiled and fell on my back. Instantly, all the lanterns in that room flared up with a mystical blue flame. On my right, there were multiple harpoons on the ceiling, arranged like a chandelier. From the ghastly object hung bodies of men, dolphins, and other fish. The dolphins were missing their trunks, the fishes their eyes, and the men - all of them were missing their limbs.

Stabbed with terror, my stomach turned and I puked, crawling away. I hit a wooden beam. I looked up to see a bunch of human feet. There must be hundreds of them. I picked myself up to look around more, and found barrels full of fish swimming in what looked like water mixed with a whole lot of blood. My legs refused to coordinate with me; helped by the turbulence of the ship, they flung me at another barrel. This was a smaller one, and it was an infant surrounded by fish eggs. "Is it alive?" Only the face of the child was visible; the rest of the body was submerged in the fish eggs. I tried to pick the baby up but failed. I couldn't hold onto it. I tried again and failed. I touched the baby's face with my fingertips - I held it, and pulled it out. It was just a head. The head of a newborn child. Darkness crept around my vision, and my head sank. I dropped the baby's head and accidentally stepped on it, crushing the skull. I slipped and fell, my vision fading out. I saw a shadow approach me. Just by the shadow, I could tell, it was Captain Vex in his shiny blue outfit, accompanied by his duelling cane. I was passing out and in my final moments, I glimpsed the captain grow in size, his cane expanding as well. A translucent glow enfolded the cane, the top split into three and formed a trident.

"Neptune…" I whispered under my breath before feeling the trident impale my gut.

~Mad Scientist

Folklore
(This serves as an epilogue for each story)

Dead Knight

Curmudgeonly the knight treads,
Along with his subsequent reluctant steps,
Bemused stood the rabble,
Eyeing the combatant, fatigued from battle,
Held a severed head insidiously in one hand,
Sword in the other,
He was a peril to no one but his father;
His kin, turns out, was king.

King

Unannounced arrived the soaring beast,
Scorching the wildlife and torching the trees.
Hurriedly fled the natives with terror,
Awaiting a hero, perhaps a sword-bearer.
Years later, an apprentice of Hermes
Slayed the dragon without any armies.

Queen

Under her reign the land bloomed
Unlike her brother freely she ruled
No family, no distraction
No famine, no starvation
The kingdom was in bliss
The chest of the queen, an Abyss

The Mind of Your Friend

"I would never even think about killing them."

Interrogator: Then why are there 37 rotting corpses in your basement?

"I didn't kill them; they starved or maybe bled to death. I just wanted their lips... I would never kill them."

Seasick

God-of the sea! God-of the sea!
Nep-tune! Nep-tune!
God-of the sea!
Bless us with for- tune, oh god Nep-tune!
Keep us afloat! Keep Zeus at bay!
Do us this and we worship every day!
Hey!
[REPEAT]

Tales From the Present

The Interview

Amber sat at the bar of an automotive-themed café sipping her latte out of a cup that was modeled after a Harley-Davidson Softail. Everything in the café was either directly or loosely inspired by an automotive entity. The seats were plain leather like old vintage cars, there were areas enclosed for friends and family. There was a van and inside of it, seating arrangements, it was for a more private company. There were small sidecars that were turned into chairs for children. The lights and lamps resembled headlights and the staff wore coveralls. The café was beside a highway, right outside the city. It was paradise for leather-wearing bike riders with glorious mustaches and other hardcore car enthusiasts. Amber was one of them. Coming from a family who has a legacy in the field of Vintage vehicles Amber was a rising enthusiast herself. Growing up, her toys were wrenches and screwdrivers. She almost stabbed her father multiple times with the screwdrivers. Just like the undying passion of her father, she followed his footsteps, not because she was forced to but because she found the dimension of automotive deeply fascinating. Her passion turned into a job when she started to write about vintage automobiles for an international magazine.

Her work led her to this engrossing café, which was oblivious to a crowd. There were barely any people in this establishment. It doesn't mean the café was unpleasant; it was a nice, warm, and a cozy café overlooking the highway. There was something magical about the headlights soaring along the road.

Amber now stood up against the giant glass window counting the headlights on the highway. She was there for an interview. She was waiting for the interviewee to arrive. She raised her arm to check the time on her wristwatch. 11:04 P.M. She had been waiting for the client since nine o'clock, she waited an entire hour before ordering a portion of pasta for herself and later, a latte to keep her awake.

"I am still here, yes, no he hasn't arrived yet. He was supposed to be here at nine... Yes, I know... Alright, love, I'll get home as soon as I am done with this. You continue with your book, can't wait to hear what you write. Okay, bye. I love you."

She hung up the phone. She smiles as she glimpses the diamond ring on her finger. The café was short on staff and many resigned due to the lack of business, it wasn't going well for the café. It seemed it was going out of business soon which was a shame, considering how pleasant the café was. A car then entered the driveway of the café. It was a vintage one, a classic. It was a 1967

Morris Minor. The car that initiated the interview in the first place. She saw it in an exhibition for such old masterpieces. It was in a corner with no spectators. Everyone seemed to ignore the car's existence and queued after Rolls-Royce's. Amber noticed the classic sit in the corner and tried contacting the owner of the car who wasn't present at the time. So she booked an interview with him at this café a week after.

"Finally, after two hours," she said under her breath "Cute car though."

Mr. Norman , the owner of the Morris mini. He gets out of his vehicle, drops the keys, bends down to pick it up, hits his head, stumbles, and falls. He gets back up and closes the door, but fingers come in between and he screams in agony. At last with sore fingers, he was able to close the car door and secure the keys in his pocket before entering the premises.

"Clumsy guy," said Amber, chugging down on the last sip of coffee, "I better get to it."

Amber saw the man through the glass interior ascending the stairs. Tripping and almost falling at every other alternate step. He reached the top and shook Amber by the hand.

"You must be Timber," said Mr. Norman confidently.

"Amber, from 'Wheels Exquisite' magazine."

"Yes yes, Amber it was, from fine exquisite cars."

Amber judged Mr. Norman heavily. He was wearing a long gray faded overcoat and a hat. He wore glasses, with smudged lenses. His trousers were stained and something odd about his boots... 'Is that...blood?'

"Anyway Mr. Norman, let's have a seat and start with the interview, it's late."

"By the devil, would you look at the time! Yes, please let's sit."

The two of them sit, and the interview commences.

"I don't like to abruptly start interviews but time is not with us, so I'll get right to it."

"Yes Miss Amber," he says, then glances at the ring on her finger, "Apologies...Mrs...Amber."

Amber puts away her hand under the table and inquires, "So how long have you had this beautiful car?"

"I bought this...this car... I mean I got this car from father. He gifted it to me not very long ago. It has been four? Five years I think... no no three, yes! Three years."

"It truly is an amazing piece; it's old, 1967, sixty-three years old! That's something."

"Yes my father took great care of the car, I- I try to do the same but I am afraid I'll get it dirty or perhaps drive it off a cliff," he said followed by maniacal laughter.

'This guy is not what I expected; he is super unprofessional, the quicker I handle this, the better.'

"Okay, tell me about th--"

"Tell me, Mrs. Amber, do you have any children?" interrupted Norman.

"Why... does that matter?" said Amber hesitantly, while slightly pressing her stomach with the palm of her hand.

"I like children," he said softly, "They are sweet and innocent, oh so, innocent."

"I had a child once, so small and tender, I just wanted to... kiss him and shower my love and and and squish him and hold him...I meant no harm..."

"Mr. Norman...are you okay?"

"Yes... Mrs. Amber, you don't have to worry"

The interview continued, Amber asked all the questions she had prepared and Norman answered each one of them unsurely and uncertainly. He stammered while answering the questions but at last, it was over.

"Thank you Mr. Norman for answering my questions and giving me your time, and I forgive you for making me wait for over two hours," she said the last part jokingly.

"I am so sorry, Mrs. Amber. So sorry. I was occupied with some...unexpected task."

Norman's eyes started to pop out as he delivered his words. He pushed on the table and stood up. A drop of red dripped down on the table from his eyes. "Oh Must have burst a vein or something" he wiped the blood off his cheek, "Come, I'll show you the car."

"I don't think that's necessary" uttered Amber with concern, "You go on home, Mr. Norman."

"HOME!? Yes...home...I remember home."

Amber looked around to scan for staff or someone but there was no one there. She peeked out of the window and spotted an employee smoking a cigarette. "Okay, I have to leave now, Good Night" Amber hurriedly collected her things and began her descent. She aggressively opened the door to find out that the employee smoking the cigarette was no longer there. She quickened her pace towards her black mini cooper but was invaded by Norman.

"Mrs. Amber. Please have a look. The car is right here."

"Alright, I don't have much time though so will take a fast survey," said Amber realizing she had no other option.

"Look look at the paint, I painted it myself, I did a few touch-ups right before coming here, here, here, see, the... the seats' pure leather finish, the steering has wooden finish." he continued to ramble on about the car till we came to the trunk.

The handle of the truck had red stains which Norman wiped hurriedly with his handkerchief. He wiped the sweat off his forehead. "Uhh, that's paint. Remember the touch-ups I did."

Amber's steps receded. The car was olive green.

"Listen, Mrs. Amber, I want to show you what I have here in my trunk."

"It's alright...I don't want to..."

Norman twisted the trunk open, revealing two faces. A mother and a child both robbed from life. The mother's dead eyes were fixed on the child and the child's eyes were at rest. The child was barely five years old. Narrow streams of blood poured out of the car's trunk and onto the driveway.

"My family..." said Norman pointing at the two corpses, "My child..."

Amber, stabbed with terror, drops the diary she held in her hand and runs towards her car. Norman stood there gawking at the two bodies laughing menacingly. "MY BABY!" he screamed.

Amber struggled to open the car door, she sat inside and ignited the engine. The engine swelled, she shifted into reverse gear and accelerated. Norman charges at the car and smashes the window. "I MISS HIM! DON'T YOU UNDERSTAND? I MEANT NO HARM! SHE WOULDN'T LET ME HOLD HIM! SHE SAID I WAS DANGEROUS!" Norman's eyes bled, veins appeared on his face and he looked truly terrifying. Amber's car jerked and was in motion. Norman fell. She shifted the car's gears and began to drive off. Through the looking glass, she saw Norman shrink before her eyes.

Amber called the police to inform them about the situation.

'A father...how can he...? His own child?' she thought, pressing her palm on her stomach again.

The next day, the news overflowed about the psychopathic murderer who had killed his own wife and son ruthlessly. He was arrested and is in custody. Amber watched the news with her partner. They hugged each other. Amber looked into his eyes. "I almost lost you", he said with clogged tears. "You won't lose me, Who would listen to your stupid stories?" They giggled amusingly before sharing a kiss.

~*Near Death*

Tooth Fairy

"Hurry up and go to sleep Jimmy. And don't forget to pack your bag for school" said Jimmy's mother calmly before closing her bedroom door.

Jimmy was a very obedient kid; he immediately packed his bag and went off to sleep. But not before he had gathered all his favorite toys by his bed and his tooth that fell off that very day, under his pillow. Later that night Jimmy had a nightmare. He was woken up by a tall slender figure with hair like thin kite strings, and a canoe-like jaw, carrying an exaggerated ominous grin. Jimmy screamed with terror only to find out his mouth was covered by the bony fingers of the mysterious figure. Eyes swimming in tears caused by the pure horror. His body was cold as ice, head light as a feather.

"Shhh" uttered the tall dark individual, while pressing one of his skinny fingers on his elaborate terrifying smile.

The creature's limbs made a cracking noise as he bent further down towards Jimmy's face. Jimmy could see the soaked-up blood on the creature's long teeth. It turned its head sideways to inspect Jimmy's face, which looked as if he was about to pass out. The creature then reached for something by its hip, a pouch. With his scrawny fingers he takes out something shiny, it glows magnificently. Jimmy screams still suppressed by its hand, his eyes blurred with the overflowing tears, he notices the glittering item in his hand. A coin. The Creature barely holding the coin properly slides it under Jimmy's pillow and takes out the tooth. It examines the tooth like a prized jewel and then impales the tooth in its chest. A drop of black blood drips from its chest to Jimmy's Blanket. It suddenly looks right into Jimmy's eyes, a child traumatized for life. Jimmy's eyes are still blurred, yet among all that water in his eyes, he sees the white glistening eyes of the creature.

"Good... Boy... Jimmy" said the creature in a stumbling voice, sounding like a possessed old man at his deathbed.

The Beast then instantly turned his face towards the window and flew outside in less than two seconds using its wings, which resembled the wings of a dead fly.

Jimmy stayed silent for a few seconds before he started screaming and bursting into tears. His parents rushed into the room with visible concern for their child. He explained the event in broken child language while sobbing uncontrollably.

"It was just a dream Honey," said his mother, "There are no such things as Monsters"

Jimmy tried to show the blood that dripped down but... gone, it wasn't there. Jimmy took out the coin from under his pillow and showed it to his parents but it still wasn't enough for them to believe the story. They consoled Jimmy till he fell asleep... or at least till he pretended to be asleep. Thinking that Jimmy slept, his parents then left the room.

Much later that very night, Jimmy opens one eye to get a peek out the window, and he sees the same tall skeletal creature staring right at Jimmy with the same exaggerated ear-to-ear grin.

Jimmy never woke up again.

~Grim Reaper

Don't Go?

So peaceful she appeared, lying in that bed. She lay there tangled with wires and pipes around her body, chest, neck, and face. The ECG machine beeped rhythmically. The room was dim, a light burned a few meters away from Mary who sat in an armchair reading a book. She was reading "It" by Stephen King; she was a huge fan of the supernatural and almost worshiped King for his masterpieces. She discovered his books at the age of nineteen and after that not a year passed by without her reading one of his books. Mary's fifteen-year-old daughter, Peach, lay on the nursing bed, she had no hair, her body was pale and she was thin as a twig. The poor child had gone through a tough childhood. Getting hit by lung cancer at the tender age of twelve she fell extremely ill. Education suffered but it didn't matter. To pursue studies, the person has to live first. Things were not in favor of Mary and Peach. The doctors give up but Mary refuses to let go. She would even spend her last dime to keep her alive as long as possible.

The cabin where Mary and Peach were situated was in a separate wing of the "Aesculapius Hospital". It was a wing where only the most serious of cases were handled, and Peach's case was one of them. There were eight cabins in this wing of the hospital and only two of them were occupied. One by Peach and the other by an old man named Jeffords. He occupied cabin five.

Mary placed a bookmark on page four hundred and thirty-seven, closed the book, and placed it on the table right beside her. She gazed at her daughter Peach, the ECG machine beeped, Mary blinked and tears formed in her eyes. She quietly sobbed and eventually wiped her tears away.

"Peach..." she whispered, "Talk to me baby."

Mary suffered from insomnia. She hasn't been able to get sound sleep for many years. Her insomnia came after the cancer. A nice, happy family of three dwindled to two after Peach's father left them. He married an Asian woman who was six years older than him and they shifted to another city. He didn't want to burden himself with the weight of a sick daughter and a sleepless mother. So he parted ways a year after cancer struck and left Mary with a mountain of responsibilities. Mary was a bank manager and had built decent financial support, but in all these years the money had shrunk significantly and is on the verge of absolute zero.

Mary gets up from her chair to pour herself a glass of water. She keeps glancing over her resting daughter hoping to see an eye flicker, or a finger move, or any kind of movement to relieve her heart. But there was nothing. Mary chugs the water and keeps the glass down when she notices movement, not her daughter, but something out the window.

Mary removed the blinds to reveal the outside world; she had been so occupied with her daughter that she had almost forgotten what the outside world looked like. It was a dark moonless night, clouds loomed above. The slight gleam among the clouds looked as if the next day the sun would rise in a maroon sky. She notices the palm tree move to and fro with the wind and she thought that the movement that she saw was most probably the tree. The window overlooked a parking lot where three cars were parked. One was at the very left corner, the other was parked right below the window and the last one was parked two spots right to the first one. Mary tried to pick out small little details in the parking lot. She saw a cat stretching in the middle of the parking lot. A street light that was supposed to illuminate the lot glowed dimly due to some faulty wiring. She shifted her gaze to the sky and said, "Good lord" she didn't know if she wanted to call it beautiful or menacing. Either way, it was a sight to behold. She closed the blinds and turned to her daughter. Still lying motionless on the bed with the ECG machine beeping beside her. She grew closer to Peach and stared at her for a few minutes replaying her childhood memories in her mind. How Peach and her father used to go to parks and play on the specific seesaw. Mary remembers the feeling that she felt when a ten-year-old peach got straight A's in all her subjects, how she came running into Mary's arms and asked for chocolate ice cream.

Memories kept playing before her eyes but it was interrupted by a change of rhythm in the ECG machine. Mary was curious to know what had changed, there was a part of her that was optimistic but mostly she was petrified. She was terrified to lose her daughter. She picked up her scarf, wrapped it around her neck and marched outside to find a nurse. The corridor's light shone weakly as well.

'Why do they have to assign us the last cabin?' thought Mary.

She quickly walked down the corridor with her eyes fixed on the ground. She kept walking and suddenly a pair of feet appeared. She closed her eyes while exhaling, preparing to unload her speech. She opened her eyes and looked up to find no one standing in front.

'What?'

She ignored the event altogether and continued her quest to find a nurse. She reached the reception where she found no one. She rang the bell on the table "Hello! Is anybody here? Hello!?"

There was a glass shield that stood before her and a telephone.

'The phone must be connected to the other wing of the hospital if I could somehow reach it I will be able to contact someone.

This hospital was a bit extra in everything, they had advanced security systems and the top-of-the-line equipment required to treat a wide range of diseases.

Mary extended her arm through the semi-circle hole in the glass shield but she was unable to reach the telephone. She tried to reach but it was just a little short. She could grab a paperweight which she threw in an attempt to get the phone within her reach, but she failed.

All of a sudden the lights turned red and a voice uttered, "Intruder alert, lockdown initiated."

A shutter dropped down which caught her arm. She screamed in agony as the shutter crushed her arm. She tried to remove it but the shutter pressed down on her arm with all its mechanical strength. She shouted for help but there was no one to be found.

"Oh god." The pain increased by the second, she pulled her arm but it did not budge, she heard her bones crack and felt her ligaments tear. She started to push with her feet which helped a little and she began to make progress. She screeched while pulling back her arm. The shutter's bottom began to feel sharp and it gradually began to cut her arm. Blood began to flow down the counter. The shutter peeled her skin as she continued to draw her hand out of there. The shoulder and her bicep were out of danger but they bled like the second day of her menstruation cycle. The elbow was the victim now. She used her legs to push but now it started to hurt more with no positive results. She had to use a different strategy. She abandoned the leg maneuver and shifted to another. With her other hand, she tried to push up the dropping shutter. Her elbow snapped and broke and she yelled as a wave of stinging pain possessed her.

"Oh my god!"

The plan didn't work flawlessly, but nonetheless, it was working. Half her arm was out. It was just the forearm and the hand which was still stuck inside. The shutter was a few centimeters away from shutting and the forearm restricted that. Mary's mental capacity had strengthened over the years. She howled as the shutter slowly peeled her skin exposing the muscles and tissues of her forearm. The nerves bulged out, they bled but Mary didn't give up, she used her legs to push. Her screams elevated; the arm began to slip out because of all the blood. She squealed one final time before her hand popped out and she fell back unconscious.

A few minutes later she opened her eyes to find herself in cabin number seven which was right opposite Peach's cabin, the lights blood red. She sat up and with blurry vision gawks at her arm. It was broken in various parts, the skin hung from her forearm, a small pool of blood beside where she lay. She was unable to lift her arm, her fingers didn't respond, and her nerves, muscles, and tissues were exposed.

A man stood in the doorway, straight. He had his long arms by his side and he stood on with his frail legs. His brown messy hair reached his shoulders but the hospital gown that he wore seemed to be crisply ironed. He didn't utter a single word and just stood there looking down on Mary. She was helpless and defeated, in desperate need of aid. The man remained immobile. The hair partially covered his eyes but the white unorganized beard and the expression that resembled a corpse were clearly visible.

Mary, realizing he was not there to help her, picked herself up and began walking back towards Peach's cabin. She approached the doorway where the man stood.

"Please move..." she requested, "My daughter...she needs me."

The man did not move an inch from his place and merely stood there looking at the pool of blood.

"Don't you understand?" Mary raised her voice, "My daughter might die."

The man lifted his head and looked directly into Mary's eyes.

"Please...Mr. Jeffords" she said softly holding her injured arm from which blood still dripped.

Jeffords tilted his head and receded, he gave way to Mary. She had her eyes locked on him as she exited the cabin. She turned her head to Peach's cabin door and hurriedly opened the door. She rushed inside, a high-pitched noise covering the room, and Peach was still laying there but with her mouth open.

"Peach, sweet child, mom is here, don't you worry," she said out loud as she brushed her bloody hand on her bald head. Tears trickled down her cheeks and she uttered, "Everything is going to be alright."

She smiled but it was short-lived, her vision became clearer and she started to notice red stains on Peach's pillow, arms, dress, sheets, and almost all of the things around her. Mary's smile turned upside down, she frowned and took a few steps back. Her eyes struggling to see properly, she shifts her head to the ECG machine that displayed a straight line. Peach lay dead. Mary fell to her knees, the dangling skin on her arm touching the floor. Time slowed down for her as she sat there in despair and denial.

A few moments later nurses rushed into the room.

"Ma'am. Can you hear me?" said an unfamiliar voice, "My name is Officer Chris."

Mary looked up to see a police officer talking. Her wound was getting dressed by a couple of nurses and she was lying down in a hospital bed.

"What...yes..." she uttered.

"She is responding," Chris informed another officer.

"What has happened?" she asked confusingly.

"Do you remember what happened here?" inquired Chris.

"I was here...with my daughter...Peach, she was ill and now..." she began to sob, "Now she is gone."

"Do you remember how?" asked softly.

"How?" asked a puzzled Mary, "How would I know that? I mean she had cancer and it took her away."

"Alright ma'am," said Chris before leaving.

The nurses continued to mend the wound as Mary stared at them doing so.

"So...does she remember?" inquired a superior officer

"It's hard to say, sir, she can be playing dumb or she just doesn't remember" answered Chris.

"It is her Chris. Jeffords saw it with his own eyes."

"How can she kill her own daughter, she spent all her money to treat her, why would she suffocate her with a pillow."

"Maybe she is a psycho, maybe she is mentally ill, or maybe it's very simple...she was tired of her...tired of taking care of something that would just leave with a snap of a finger."

The word of the superior officer baffled Chris and he didn't want to believe any of them.

Time passed. The environment was in mayhem but among all that chaos Officer Chris gazed at Mary who sat with a bandaged arm with a smirk on her face. The same smirk he saw in the "Lyssa Assylum" on a woman who killed her three children.

~Exhaustion

The Whispering

"I don't believe in the supernatural but that day I was forced to think otherwise."

I live in a town where people sleep at eight o'clock, it is possibly one of the most boring towns one can ever be born in. It was my top priority to earn a fortune and get out of this wretched place. I had a brother which was the only thing that was making my stay at this hellhole somewhat tolerable. I even found my parents dull and tedious.

I struck the lottery when I found out that I had found a job in the city and it even pays well. I was overjoyed at this news until my bubble popped when I read that I needed to reach the office at seven in the morning. The town was miles away from the city and the fastest way there was the train. I made myself familiar with the train schedules and saw that a train briefly halts at my town's station for five minutes before leaving for the city. The stoppage occurs at precisely 5:30 A.M. It is roughly a twenty-minute walk from my house to the train station which wasn't the issue. The problem was I had to wake up at around four o'clock, get ready for work, and rush to the train station. I will have to make this my routine until I can afford to pay rent in the city and stay away from this place.

I did this for a solid five months and started to build some financial stability. I was ready to shift to the city. I scoured the internet for places I could rent and found a beautiful little place near a children's park. It wasn't a big apartment but it was exactly what I was looking for. A compact personal space to continue my journey further. Gradually I moved all my necessary stuff from the town to my apartment and just out of pure formalities decided to stay in the house one last night before totally shifting to the city.

It was the crack of winter; the sun didn't rise until around six in the morning. I hated waking up so early and immediately forcing my body to work. Occupational hazard. I couldn't sleep due to the sheer thrill of leaving this place forever the next day.

My phone dinged, which broke my almost light sleep. My body spasmed and I jolt myself awake. "This is it, time to leave this awful place." I tried to wake my brother up but he was a deep sleeper. I did bid them farewell before they went to sleep but my heart still wanted to speak to my brother. I convinced my heart not to do it. I grabbed my things, looked at my brother most probably for the last time in a very long time, and left the house. I made sure that the door was locked and I was on my merry way.

It was dark, very dark. There was no moonlight-- even If there was a moon in the sky it was hidden by the clouds. I had a handy flashlight that my brother had gifted me. I was walking through the tall wheat fields my family owned and quickly found myself on the path that would take me to the train station. There was something oddly uncanny about today. I felt heavier, even though I had fewer things on me. Most of my stuff was already in the apartment. Yet I felt this almost unbearable weight on my shoulders. It was like someone was pushing me down. I quickened my pace, breathing faster, my arm hair rising then falling back. On the brink of a panic attack, I noticed someone in the distance. Illuminated by the shine of my flashlight the figure appeared dark. 'A companion!', I thought to myself. "Hey man?! Wait up" I screamed at the mysterious figure. I tried not to flash my light on the person thinking it would be weird if I do so-- I tried to approach them. "Are you going to the train station as well?" I tried making conversation, "If yes, then I am going the same way, just hold on for me." I desperately wanted them to wait for me so I can get a partner to walk with and get rid of the spooky feeling. After walking for about a minute I reached the point where they stood but I raised my torch to find out that the figure seemed to have teleported to a distance.

"Wha- How did- Hey! Wait up man!" I screamed "Don't run away from me!"

I started to walk faster as my shoulders began to feel heavier than ever. I started gaining on the peculiar figure. I started to sweat in the freezing temperature and another bizarre thing began. I started to hear someone whispering. I turn my head around to check, but no one. I continue my journey and the whispering grows more noticeable. I turn my head again to find no one. "Is my mind playing tricks with me?" I thought to myself but even my thoughts were suppressed by the strange whispering sound that filled my ears. I almost reached the person and from this range, I could figure out that the person was a woman dressed in all black. The dress was ripped, the drapes were drenched, and even under the light of my torch, she didn't appear clearly.

"Ma'am, I asked you to wait up," I said with a sigh, my ears still bursting with whisperings. "Also do you hear that too?"

The whispering abruptly stopped. I felt a quiet calm. A relief but a brief one.

"Excuse me Ma'am I am talking to you," I said while walking beside her, "Are you going to the station too?"

It was like talking to a moving wall; she didn't say anything and continued to walk. Her face was partially covered with a piece of cloth; only her eyes were visible. I couldn't focus on her eyes too much, it was dark and impossible for me to see and describe anything clearly. We were walking together towards the station when gradually I started to feel the same pressure on my shoulders. The whispering returned as well.

"Are you scared?" uttered the lady, "You seem scared..."

I felt chills run down my body as those words entered my ears mixed with the unbearable whisperings.

I stuttered, "What- Scared? Me? No no... Why would I be scared?"

"Are you sure? You look... terrified."

It seemed all the blood on my face had vanished and I grew pale by the second. I tried not to freak out but on the inside, I was screaming.

"I am not 'terrified'. There is no need to be."

"Let me show you something then," she said, raising her arm from the side, removing the cloth that surrounded it, and revealing her arm.

Under the glow of my flashlight, I observed her arm. The arm was burnt into a crisp and it looked like it had been struck by a machete multiple times. Terror-struck I stumbled destabilizing my flashlight which then shone on her face. For a brief moment, the cloth that wrapped her face rippled and my eyes glanced at her jaw which appeared scorched as well. The whispering grew, and so did my pace of walking. I was a level down from jogging. I struggled to keep up the pace but right by my side, the woman had no issue catching up with me. It was as if she was levitating rather than walking.

"Do you want to see my face?"

I was horrified and had no will to even answer that question but my self-defense mechanism triggered and I said, "Yes... sure... not here though. It's too dark here. In the station. Else I'll be late for the train."

"Did you not see the time... before wandering out in the night?"

"Excuse me...?" I take out the phone from my pocket. The displayed time on my phone was staring back at me and I felt like an absolute fool. It was 3:00 A.M. on the dot. I didn't care to check the time before leaving the house. My desperation to leave the house forever was so significant that I ignored the concept of time. 'Would this lead to my death? Snap out of it!'

I could see the train station in the distance and my mind just wanted to teleport to the station or perhaps to my house besides my brother. The Whisperings became deafening and the woman's voice began to echo around my head.

"Let me show you my face."

"Sure, let's just reach the station first."

Her pace started to recede as the station grew near. The whisperings slowed down but still bounced around my head. The situation seemed to be going in my favor until I felt suffocated, it was like I was drowning, I was familiar with this feeling before. Ten years old. Family picnic at the local lake. Someone pushed me. Brother? I couldn't afford to slow down but my body refused to keep up the speed. I fell to my knees grabbing my neck, struggling to breathe. The whisperings faded but did not disappear. I resisted looking behind but like a reflex, my head turned. I flashed my torch back in her direction and saw her hovering in the air. All the clothes were rippling and flying, but there was no wind. Her eyes, blood red, popped out of her sockets. She extended her arms sideways which resembled a cross before screaming at the top of her lungs resulting in me looking away. I was so close to the station. I closed my eyes and crawled in that direction till I felt a hand on my head.

I open my eyes, blurry due to how tightly I had closed them. I saw a man, with no legs, a homeless person, who seemed to have a corner in the station where he lived.

"There, There, You are alright." said a homeless person.

"YOU HAVE TO HELP ME THERE IS THIS WOMAN WHO WHO-", I realize that all the whispering along with the mysterious woman had disappeared.

"I know what it is child, come, I'll tell you."

I followed the elderly man to his corner where I sat and was able to breathe properly.

"I see that you have met Agatha," said the old man passing me a bottle of water.

I chug the water in one go and say "What? Who is that?"

"That's Agatha you see; she is one of the women who died on that path, a few months ago. She was killed by a group of assaulters who did what they had to do with her then chopped and burned her body."

I stare at the old man with skepticism and ask "How...do you know about this? Doesn't she attack you?"

"Well, you see, child. I tried to protect poor Agatha from the assaulters, but as you can see..." he said emphasizing his missing legs, "I failed... They cut off my legs and threw me away. By God's grace, I survived, but poor Agatha wasn't that lucky."

I listened to the man's story with undivided attention as he went on explaining and ranting about the various girls who had fallen victim to those assaulters. Not every girl's soul was as powerful as Agatha's hence all their souls were just able to whisper. Make us aware of their existence. Want to tell their stories? Wanting justice.

"I hear them every night, whispering in my ears. I see Agatha in the distance. I pray for her, that all I can do... that's all a poor homeless man can do." He said before breaking down into tears.

I tried to console him, but I made little to no difference. I contemplated my thoughts, and collected them till the train arrived at 5:30 A.M. I took that train to the city and never looked back. I stayed far away from that town. I was a different man after what happened that night, I became more passionate about safety but at the same time, I had a fear of losing my limbs. I adopted a low-key life, not wanting to be the hero that my heart desired. I listened to my mind, probably not the best decision that I have made but one that would keep me out of the drama.

~Sexual Harassment

Fiction

"I am sick of you! I will not tolerate any sort of blabbering, useless, sheets of toilet paper in this house", screamed Linda

Zoey barges out of the house, away from her screaming mother. Without a drop of tear in her eyes and her head held high, she marched forward. She carried a couple of books, her hair tied to a bun with a pencil poked into it, a dull skirt, and a mucky shirt. There were pen marks on her smooth white skin, and in some places scars caused by domestic violence.

Her father was a drunk and her mother a drug addict. They lived in a small wrecked place where the roof barely held together. Linda was a massive Meth head and she along with her partner drains all their money on addictions they cannot control. Linda's husband Casper did nothing for a living, they were thieves, and they were the lowest of the social class. Yet they birthed the bright and beautiful Zoey. Linda often brought money selling her body to random strangers for a while and Casper stole from pedestrians.

Zoey was in the wrong family, she was different from her parents, and she had a passion to read and write. It was a mystery how she adopted the habit, but nonetheless, it was one that would differentiate her from her insane parents. When she was fourteen years old her body was marked red with all the beating of her father. She found something under the bed where she hid. A half-torn book. 'The Hobbit.'

It always wasn't like this. They were once a happy family, it was when she was born. A few years later everything fell apart after they were introduced to the dreadful drug. Zoey's education was halted, they used the same money to buy alcohol and methamphetamine. A bright mind like Zoey's was being wasted in an environment so toxic. Until she developed a mind of her own and was capable enough to revolt against her oppressing parents.

At fourteen she read half of J.R.R. Tolkien's 'The Hobbit' was mesmerized by the imagination and ambiguity of the text and when she turned to the ninety-seventh page of the novel, she was left unsatisfied. There were no more pages for her to read, they were missing. Off she went on a quest to find the rest of the story. She searched her house but was unable to find it. Her expedition expanded and she set her foot outside to search for the unfinished story. Her quest brought her in front of an old building. A clock in the middle right on top, two towers on two ends, and a grand gate, big enough to allow a small elephant to pass through. The town's library. She entered the majestic building that carries thousands of stories, not just inside the books it holds but also the very walls of the structure. The first time, she felt this is where she belongs.

Now, at twenty-four, the same feeling embraces her every time she sets foot inside the enchanting premises. The reception counter was a long wooden table where an old woman sat with her thick glasses and an Agatha Christie book in her possession. She eyes as Zoey entered and her face immediately produced a smile.

"Hello again dear, did you finish the Mistborn trilogy?" asked the old woman carrying a sweet smile.

"I haven't even reached halfway through the second book Mrs. Darla!" she exclaimed, "My parents are being extra annoying lately."

"It's okay my dear, take your time. It is a true marvel of a series. Brandon Sanderson is a genius."

"That we can both agree on Mrs. Darla, unlike Shakespeare, I still don't know what you see in his writings."

They both chuckled at the statement as Zoey registered her name in the register. The last twenty-six entries were all Zoey, there was just one other name, Franco, who visited three weeks ago, interestingly he didn't register his exit. Probably forgot and left in a hurry.

Zoey placed the pen on the counter, waved at Mrs. Darla, and entered the main hall. She drank water from the old water dispensary which was placed just beside the hall's entrance. The hall stretched with ancient bookshelves filled with books and Papers bound up together. Zoey brushed her fingers through the spines of the books as she moved forward. She stopped when she noticed 'Fellowship of the Ring' plastered on one of the spines. She smiled and then made her way towards the desk. It was her spot, this is where she has spent the last ten years, reading, learning, and most importantly losing herself in stories. Transporting herself away from her grim reality to the lush lands of 'Middle earth' in Tolkien's 'The Lord of the Rings, the gothic environment of 'Wuthering Heights', the magical universe of 'Harry Potter', the frightening corridors of the overlook hotel in Stephen King's 'The Shining' and various other places. She was a very versatile reader; she was a fan of almost all genres. She wasn't picky and displayed curiosity in everything. Although she strongly preferred reading fiction she did not have any major issues with non-fiction works. The only minor issue was that she found them boring, hence she stuck with fiction.

She sat at her desk reading the second book in the Mistborn trilogy, to find out why the harmless mist has started to kill people. She heard a sound emerge from the extreme back.

'Was that a roar?' she thought to herself 'Is there an animal here?'

She continued to read but was distracted again by the same noise. It sounded like an animal. This time, it scared Zoey, her head felt lighter and her heartbeat quickened. Adrenaline rushed into her blood and she got up to go investigate the source of the sound. She placed her foot one after the other looking carefully in the distance, her eyes fixed on one particular bookshelf. The sound swelled. She felt the ground vibrate as she approached the alleged bookshelf. She placed her hand beside the shelf and peeked around. There was nothing there. Just another alley dimly lit, with books on both sides. She sighed and turned around to go back to her desk. She walked back to her desk, constantly looking behind her, feeling paranoid about someone's presence. She reached her desk and gazed at the book she was reading. It was drenched in blood. A blob of what looked like a human liver was placed on top of the book and drops of blood dripped down the desk. Stabbed with terror her steps receded, her palm pressed on her open mouth. Thanks to her parents she has seen many obscure sights but this was beyond anything she had ever seen and it was just the beginning of the horrible nightmare. She walked back without looking and stepped on someone's feet. She turned to see a very tall man, close to six and a half feet standing with his chest pumped and he wore a charming smile.

"I will save you young woman!" he shouted, "There is nothing to fear!"

He smiled after delivering those words and Zoey looked at him with utter confusion. His smile increased and kept increasing till his cheeks started to tear. His lips tore as well. They bled heavily, along with his eyes which were clogged with blood. His pupils disappeared, his facial skin began to peel off by itself and his head grew in size. Zoey stood there baffled at sight watching the head fill up like a balloon and eventually, it popped. It splattered blood all over and stained Zoey's white shirt.

"What the hell?!" she said, dumbstruck.

She heard a crackling sound. Something heavy was walking on the weak wooden floor of the library. The shelves vibrated and books fell. Zoey stabilizes herself, and prevents herself from falling because of the spinning head of hers. She looked up to find a claw emerging from top of the shelves.

"A...Dinosaur?" she whispered

Then the nose of the dragon appeared, blowing smoke out. It climbed up the shelf revealing its golden scales that moved like the tail of a rattlesnake. The dragon spread its wings and growled at Zoey. She fell back, her gaze fixed on the dragon as it was about to rain fire on her.

A yell shifted and made her eyes shift to the right, a group of Achaean warriors wielding spears and shields rushed the dragon. The dragon fell as they attacked and impaled the dragon with their weapons. One of the Achaeanian soldiers approached Zoey and said, "We will handle this now. Troy will fall!"

Zoey's mind was unable to comprehend. One moment ago she was in a library that no one visited, and the other she was in Homer's 'The Iliad'. The Dragon hissed, its three-forked tongue slithered out which was then sliced by Achilles. What was he doing there? Zoey had no clue. The beast that oddly looked just like the description of the dragon in Ovid's Metamorphoses, was defeated. The instant the dragon fell, worms and bugs appeared on the dragon's skin and devoured its flesh. The beast's body swollen with venom burst, splattering it everywhere, killing the worms.

Zoey ran.

She ran to get out of the library but she was greeted by mist during her desperation to find the exit. Was it the mist from a Stephen King book or was it from 'Mistborn'? Without a thought in her mind, she ran into the mist as it swirled around her. She ran straight for two minutes straight, the library was big, but not big enough to be running for two minutes and not find something to hit. She halted to take deep breaths. She panted and coughed. An ominous sound called her name from behind. She looked back to find a 'Mistwraith', *a creature composed only of soft tissue, who consumes the bones of several other creatures, which they then use as their own skeleton.*

"Brandon Sanderson you monster!" she screamed, "Why must you create something like this?"

She sprinted in the opposite direction till she was out of the mist. Just when she exited the mist, she came across a group of elderly people all seated in chairs forming a circle. There were around ten of them, one of which was Mrs. Darla. She sat in the middle. All of them had put their serious faces on and had not a glimpse of amusement.

"Excuse me?" Zoey said politely, "Mrs. Darla?"

All of them except Darla stood at once and turned their heads away from Zoey. Their bodies twisted and faced Zoey, who was terror-stricken. Their head a hundred and eighty degrees turned and they slowly moved towards a frightened Zoey. She closed her eyes tightly, covered her ears with her hands, and screamed her lungs out. She felt a push from behind which knocked her to her knees. She opened her eyes after a few seconds of screaming and removed her hands from her ears. She had something in her hands. Her body shivered and she grinded her teeth. She had her hands clutching something. She gawked at her fists and saw signs of blood. She slowly loosened her fists to reveal her palms, and in those palms laid her ears, torn from their places. A high-pitched noise embraced her head and her vision began to fade.

She was about to pass out when a pair of hands shook her grabbing her shoulders.

"Was machst du Soldat?" (What are you doing soldier?") said a uniformed man with a red band around his arm.

"Runter! Runter!" (Run! Run!) screamed a similarly dressed man from a distance.

Zoey looked around her, perplexed again. She was on a battlefield. Soldiers, barbed wires, dead horses, complex old machinery, tanks, and vehicles on fire, surrounded her. The sky was gray and gloomy. The air choked with smoke, and the world turned monochrome, except for the blood and fire which burned a fiery red.

Zoey was tackled down by a man who shouted "Granate ankommen!" (Grenade incoming!)

Zoey felt her ribs break and her chest fill up with internal bleeding. She gasped for air, but all she could inhale was smoke and gunpowder. She was getting suffocated, she was dying, slowly but surely.

The man that tackled her down also had a red band around his arm. He stood back up, reloaded his gun and chanted, "Wir müssen kämpfend sterben! Für ihn! Für Führer!" (We must die fighting! For him! For Fuhrer!) before getting shot by a sniper three hundred meters away from him.

Zoey passed out.

"Darling? Can you hear me dear?" uttered a familiar voice.

Zoey tried to open her eyes, but she struggled to do so, but ultimately was able to do it. She squinted and noticed Mrs. Darla by her side. She was lying in an ambulance with wires strapped to her body.

"What happened?" she somehow mumbled from her dry lips.

"Oh thank sweet god!" said Mrs. Darla, placing her hand on her chest. "What a relief!"

Zoey smiled, not because she was alive, but because someone was there for her. Someone who was overwhelmed with her survival. Someone who cared about her.

"It was this Franco dear...he was living in the library, among the hundreds of bookshelves. He had been there three weeks. Eating pages, pieces of wood, and even his own flesh. He was a drug addict, the worst one you will ever see. Even worse than your parents child He mixed lethal doses of something called 'LSD' in the water that you drank."

Zoey listened with her eyes closed, her smile expanding with every word Mrs. Darla said.

"I wanted to check on you and give you the cookies I made this weekend, but upon entering the hall, I sensed a foul smell. So I investigated and found Franco. Naked. Tearing books, cutting his flesh, and munching on them. He was an animal...even animals are more civilized than him. I called the police and they responded. It was quite hard to catch him as he went wild and hustled all over the library. But after four officers got scratched and bitten by him, they finally caught that vile creature. They have taken him away."

Mrs. Darla noticed Zoey's smile to which she asked, "Why are you smiling dear?"

A drop of tear trickled down Zoey's cheek and she responded, "It wasn't real Mrs. Darla...Thank god all of that wasn't real."

~Back to Reality

White Mask

"Where am I? Open the blindfold, please... If you want money, we have plenty. Just stop this madness.", Screamed a terrified man sitting in a chair, tied up.

Footsteps approached. The man fell silent.

"If you think it is money that I want, then you, my friend, are deeply mistaken. I do not want your money. In fact, I have no use keeping you here." Said a deep voice growing closer to the tied-up man.

"Just let me go then."

"You think everything is so simple, don't you Dan? But let me tell you darling the world is a bitter place. No one gets their way just by being simple. Like me, all those years ago. A simple, sober, innocent... stupid, dumb, waste of a human being", he put his hands on both of Dan's shoulders.

"What are you talking about? WHY THE HELL AM I HERE!?", shouted Dan.

The mysterious guy turns the chair and blows a punch right in Dan's gut. Dan's spine bends forward followed by an uncontrollable cough. He struggled to breathe.

"You see Dan! That is your problem! That foul mouth of yours. Ever since you were a little kid. The annoying little spoiled brat, living in a mansion, spending all your father's fortune. No wonder he left...", his voice fading.

"How- do you know—about my family so much?" He coughed in between. What I do is my business. What is it to you coward?", Dan looked up to his face and even though he had a blindfold on, it seemed he saw right through it.

"You call me a coward? Oh, darling...Was it me who killed an unarmed, blameless girl in your father's Audi? You were done with her! So the first thing that crossed your mind was to end a life that was not yours to claim! It is such an effortless job, isn't it? Being rich, not with your own blood and sweat pouring into passions, obsessions, and into every idea that enters the mind of a hard worker. No... you got it all easy, you were born rich. Useless! Without the guardians of a father. Useless! Without the care of a mother. Useless! Without a generous heart. It's all...Useless.

"I don't have to explain my crimes to you...whoever you are. You don't know me. I am Dan Hoyot. Do you even know what that name means?" uttered Dan with arrogance in his tone.

"Oh it is true...the money takes the brain away. Do you even realize the irony in what you said?" he takes off

Dan's blindfold, and the overhead light shone brightly into Dan's eyes. A few seconds later his eyes adjusted and he saw a man in a sharp suit wearing a plain white mask that covered his entire face.

"What is this? Who are you? What V for Vendetta shit is this?"

White mask stood there elegantly with his hands in his pocket. He was a sleek man, tall, and had regal body language. He took out a pocket knife from his chest pocket and grew closer to Dan. Pointing the tip of the blade towards Dan he uttered.

"Tell me, darling, What did you do to your mother?"

Dan's face froze, it went numb.

"Tell me"

"I didn't do anything, She had a heart attack okay?

White mask clutches the handle of his knife and buries it deep in Dan's knee.

Dan screamed and grunted. "You stupid bastard!"

"Look at me!" said white mask loudly while grabbing his face, then softly, "If I take the knife out, you will bleed. So for now we keep the knife...okay?

Dan ground his teeth and breathed heavily.

White mask placed a chair and as he sat he said, "Alright. Let me tell you a story."

"Shut up you son of a---"

Dan was interrupted; the white mask pushed the blade deeper into his knee.

Agony wrapped Dan and their eyes shed tears.

"You will listen. And be a good boy. Unlike how you have been all your life."

Dan looked at white mask with rage and fury burning on top of his head.

"Alright, story time. Dan! Do you remember the time when you brought a girl into your lush mansion?"

"I bring a bitch to my place every other day, Which one are you talking about?" said Dan grinding his teeth.

"Who managed your manners, Dan? Your mother did not, that's for sure. If she did, you wouldn't have done what you did to her a few days ago. SHE WAS YOUR DAMN MOTHER! But you Dan were Oedipus! All those girls that you brought into your expansive mansion were not enough!"

"Let me get out of here man... and I will handle you." Dan leaned forward.

"Just like you 'handled' all those innocent lives? Did you spare any of them?"

"You won't get it, I did what I had to do. What mother got? She deserved it. After what she did, or well, after what she did NOT do. She was never a mother, I never saw her around. We lived and breathed in the same house, and I only saw her like twenty times in my entire life. She was like every other woman to me."

"I know how you see every other woman. An object. Someone that you can use. Someone without any lives of their own. You are so self-centered that you don't care, it doesn't even cross your mind that every girl has a life, family, ambitions, plans, and much more."

"Why do you care?" smiled Dan.

"It's right..."

Dan nodded his head and laughed maniacally. "Tell me the story that you were telling."

White mask's eyes didn't move, half closed, it was fixed on Dan's face.

"Once I was walking down the beach at night, listening to my favorite tunes. Gathering confidence to meet some people. It was my first time in the city. And there I see... a white jeep rolling towards the sea. I turned my music off and got closer. I hear screams so I decide to hide by the shed. I peek over and see you and in your arms a girl, with a slit throat. I saw her body twitch, it was fresh. And then I saw you carry her over your head and scream 'This is for you the god of the ocean' and chuck her body into the sea. You laughed and laughed so much, I saw the amusement in your eyes. It was so funny for you."

Dan chuckled.

"You are still laughing..." The white mask takes out the knife from his knee.

Dan doesn't make a sound.

"From that point onwards I kept a close eye on you, Dan. I saw the girl you buried in your five-acre garden, the girl you threw from the skyscraper downtown which was on the news by the way. 'The girl that fell from heaven' was another interesting one, little do they know you threw her from your helicopter. And a bunch of girls who were found in dumpsters all around the city. I have seen you kill every girl from that point onwards. I know what you did to them before, and just after you were done, the dagger came out, or a gun, a knife, whatever you had available at that time. Out of curiosity, why did you kill them? Why not use them more and more until they are worn out?"

Dan looked up, perplexed. "I don't like to reuse things, I don't even wear one t-shirt more than once. But I also don't let any other person wear that t-shirt. The same thing applies to my women."

White mask sighed.

Dan keeps looking at him and inquires. "If you saw me do all that...why didn't you stop me...?"

White mask puts his palm on the back of his neck and says, "Are you kidding me? That shit was fun as hell. You and I are not so different Dan. It is the proudest I have felt in years, to see you defile women and then straight up take their lives. That was amusing and arousing at the same time. You have made me proud son, good job following your father's footsteps."

"What? Dad?" uttered a confused Dan.

He takes off his mask revealing his face. "Yes darling, it's me."

Dan's face went pale as if he saw a ghost.

"All those years ago at my young age, I used to do the same things. Glad to see you doing it way better than me. But then one time, I fell in love with a woman, she was beautiful, subtle and just the one for me... that woman was your mother...whom you—" Hoyot's voice cracked. "You choose to kill her Dan. And not only just kill but..., she was the love of my life Dan, and she was your mother for god's sake!"

"Where were you? I was ten when you left! Poof! You were gone for fourteen years and suddenly decided to come back?" asked Dan.

"I relapsed Dan. I was thirsty for more of my young-age endeavors. I loved how each drop of blood dripped down their bare bodies: used, helpless, innocent, such a turn-on. But after fourteen more years of that, I was done. I realized I have stayed away from your mother for too long, so I decided to come back. And what do I see on the beach the first day, you. I delayed my meeting until you crossed the line. Until you killed the love of my life."

"What now..." asked Dan softly.

"You die. Obviously." Hoyot went behind a tied-up Dan and gently sliced his throat. He pats the shoulder of a suffering Dan and says, "Shouldn't have taken her from me, Dan. Everything was so good! You just had to mess everything up! I can't watch you die, after all, you are still my son."

Hoyot takes out a revolver from his side holster, places it on the side of his head, and pulls the trigger. Parts of Hoyot's brain splatter and his body falls with a thud. His sharp suit was stained with flowing blood. Dan bled as time went ahead, his vision began to black out and in a few minutes, he died.

~Karma

"I Do"

"I do", said Jess with a graceful smile..

"And Haytham do you take Jess as your lawfully wedded wife?" asked the pastor.

"I do", Haytham matched the same smile on Jess's face.

"By the power vested in me by the State, I pronounce you husband and wife, You may kiss the bride."

Haythem leans in and they share a beautiful kiss. A room full of strangers broke into a round of applause. Haytham and Jess looked each other in the eyes tearing up. They had done it, through all the ups and downs they had finally emerged victorious. Haythem lost himself in her eyes, reminiscing the first time they met. How wonderfully the pieces fell into place.

It was a dark moonless night and on the side of the highway stood helpless Haythem, he looked around to find no one. His 2008 Honda civic was smoking at the edge of the road, the bonnet boiling of the overheated car. The desert was unforgiving, dehydration already kicked in after four hours of walking aimlessly. The sun went down and the cool evening breeze took over. This was the only time Haythem scouted for passing cars. Other times he hated that anyone other than him owned and drove a car. Humming to his favorite songs he treads lightly gazing into the horizon, without a single sign of human civilization. He was optimistic and held his head high even though all hope seems lost. His knees ached, and his hair flew with the creeping cold wind of the desert. More time passed, his legs barely holding up, and he gasped for air. But the air contained sand and dust which he coughed out.

"This is how I die...at least young and still moderately attractive" he chuckled.

"Sarcasm huh?" whispered a woman.

Haythem turned and screamed, "Holy mother of god!"

"It's okay", she said raising her arms and trying to calm him down "I mean no harm."

"How did you do? Where? What?" mumbled a perplexed Haythem.

"That's not the question you want to ask me..." she replied hopping around him.

Haythem turned his head to catch her in his sight but she playfully kept dodging his eyes.

"If you are a sand wraith or a ghost just kill me now, do not torture me or feed my limbs to your children", said Haythem looking up at the sky with his hands joined together.

"That's stupid" the woman stopped, "Look at me."

Haythem turns his gaze down to notice a white face, ashen-haired woman perhaps no more than his age. The night was surely moonless, but Haythem just discovered his moon.

"My name is Jess," she said extending her arm for a handshake.

"Uh...Haythem" he stuttered.

"You seem unsure..." her face turned gloomy, and her amusement faded, "Is that really your name...? Or did you kill someone and took his identity, because if you did that...I would know" she came closer to his face as she delivered these lines.

"Uh...ma'am I just wanna get out of here, back to my life, I don't want to die...please."

Jess's face lit up and she burst into laughter, "You should have seen your face, so tense yet tender" she continued to laugh.

Haythem took a deep breath and forced a smile, "Haha, I knew that."

"Did you now?" she chuckled, "Do you know that I am about to rip your throat and feast on it right now."

"Umm...no?" Haythem said hesitantly.

"Good! Because that's not what I am thinking dummy" she laughed and hopped around him again.

"Phew...why are you so energetic? Wait, that's not the question. How are you so energetic?"

"Can't a girl be jolly?" she questioned, "In the middle of a desert just mind her own business till I ran into you."

"Are you sure you 'ran' into me", Haythem raised an eyebrow, "The chances of that happening are quite slim taking all things into consideration."

"Oh shut up!" she thundered, "You are dying, let me help you, my car is that way."

"The lady has a car!" he screamed with joy, "Of course you do, god has finally blessed me."

"Bit dramatic don't you think?"

"Try walking in the desert for, I don't know, seven hours? You'll know."

"Trust me I have spent a much longer time in the desert than you."

"What?" he raised a brow again.

"Oh come on! You are such a baby! Come, we go to my car" she said skipping away.

"Jeez! This girl is full of energy" he whispered.

"I heard that!" she said.

'What! How?' he thought.

Jess skipped and hopped humming a tune. Haythem was too far away from her to hear what she hummed. He occasionally had to jog to catch up to her. He noticed her gray hair dimly glistening. It was like a silver lining in his cloud of hopelessness. He got close enough to recognize the song she was humming. It was "Brain

Damage", the same song he was humming moments earlier. He wondered if it was her favorite song, but was too dehydrated to get into that conversation.

"That's the car over there" she pointed with her index finger.

Haythem looked over and spotted a jet-black SUV with a siren on top.

"That's your car?" Haythem asked frowning.

"Yes...is there a problem?"

"Seems like a vehicle for feds, or maybe military people."

"Umm... it's my brother's car and yes you are correct, he is in the special forces."

Things fell out of place for Haythem. He was skeptical of the entire situation but whenever he turned his gaze to Jess, his heart skipped a beat and his speech stumbled. Even in all the darkness, he saw her face clearly.

"You are...beautiful" Haythem said softly.

Jess blushed, she unlocked the car and said, "Get inside, I have water on the dash."

Haythem hurried inside the car and chugged the entire bottle of water at once.

"Easy there," she said, sitting beside him in the driver's seat.

She began to drive along the gigantic dunes, the handling of the car was quite awful, and she was clearly not a good driver. Haythem drank all the water available in the car. After every move, his eyes glanced at Jess. It wasn't him doing it purposely but it was just his heart being pulled toward her. It was irresistible. His palms were sweating and he became extra aware of the surroundings. His senses were enhanced and he could even feel that there were two flies in the car. Among the chaos and turbulence of the vehicle, he asked, "Is there something in the trunk?"

She turned her head with superhuman speed, opening her eyes wide open and spoke, "In the trunk? Yeah I have supplies...my brother's supplies."

"Your supplies or your brother's?"

"Both our supplies", she said quickly.

Haythem didn't care about what lay in the car's trunk; he was just trying to avoid the overwhelming emotion that he felt. He changed topics from stuff in the trunk to how hot the sun's surface is, to how ants never sleep. But none of them changed the fact that four freshly executed corpses lay behind the closed door of the trunk. Their throats were ripped out.

Haythem fell asleep in the car while having a conversation with Jess. They discovered human civilization in a distant town named "Elanda" from where Haythem found assistance to go back home.

After the incident, Jess and Haythem didn't separate, rather they grew closer. Although even after eight months Haythem knew the bare minimum about Jess's life, he was madly in love with her and so was she. Without any family to wait for, the two got married in a church on a Sunday where many devotees witnessed the wedding. It was wonderful, the collision of two beings in such a strange circumstance led to them swearing not to leave each other's side till eternity.

"I thought your brother would at least attend your wedding Jess", he said removing his tie, "I didn't know stealing his car for that one night would affect him so much."

"Well yeah", she said softly, "I can't help it..."

"I am sure he would regret it later."

"What about your family?" she questioned, "Why didn't they attend?"

"I told you Jess!" he exclaimed, "I ran away from my family and I am never looking back, It's better off from that drug addict of a family."

They both shied away while talking about their families, a natural effect of lying to someone you love. He changed his clothes while she removed her makeup; they both did something to evade making eye contact. But for how long?

Jess's hands stopped and she stood up from the chair facing the mirror. She gazed at Haythem from the mirror with tears forming in her eyes and said, "Haythem..."

He turns to look at her and spoke, "Yes? "

"This is the beginning of something beautiful and I don't want to start this with a monstrous lie", her voice cracked, "I want to show you something."

She grabbed his arm and pulled him out to the balcony. It was a full moon that shone brightly amidst clouds scattered around it.

"What is it?" Haythem frowned.

Jess took a few steps back and looked up. She extended her arms high up in the air and uttered, "Doamne, transformă-mă" (Lord, Transform me).

The clouds partially covering the moon vanished. Jess's legs grew, her calves had a joint, ashen hair appeared on her whole body, her arms became slender yet extremely long, her chest puffed out, her pupils dilated, followed by her chin splitting into two.

Haythem stood there without moving a muscle, stiff as a tree.

Jess's nose shrunk, her back made a noise resembling the cracking of bones, and her long slender arms blossomed a fine pair of razor-sharp claws.

"This is me..." she said in a demonic voice, "I am a walking curse."

Haythem didn't say a word for a while, and then he scratched his head and said, "Why didn't you tell me earlier?"

Jess looked into Haythem's eyes that intently dodged her eyes.

"I was afraid to lose you", she said, trying to make him look at her, "Did I lose you?"

Haythem casually puts his hand on his shoulder and peels off his skin.

Jess was perplexed at the scene but soon she realized that Haythem was not human as well.

After the removal of his human skin, he revealed his glaringly pale silver body, his eyes as big as a billiards ball, his nose as sharp as a knife, and his tongue splitting into three. An extraterrestrial. A runaway from a distant planet. Cast out from his people for showing an unacceptable amount of interest in planet earth.

"Not so different after all" he smiled before embracing her with his abnormally long arms.

~Not what you expect

Victim Trilogy

Chauffeur

I generally don't drive all night but desperate times call for desperate measures. The Doctor has found signs of a tumor in my head and all I want to do now is drink till alcohol flows in my veins. To do that though, I needed money, lots of it and my sub-par boring day job wasn't providing the adequate amount of funds to do so. Hence I started this side hustle chauffeuring people around.

In the twomonths I had spent driving, I didn't care about the passengers, not even a little bit. All I was interested in was money. Never spoke to any of them even if they tried to talk to me. They ended up feeling uncomfortable and just stayed silent for the rest of the trip. There were also many passengers who I was interested in; they consisted mostly of teenage girls going to a hotel after a busy night of clubbing. I wouldn't say I was a creep but peeking at their bodies through the looking glass instantly aroused me unlike with my aged wife back home. The sheer amount of people making out in the back seat was immense. I never intentionally looked to pick up people that would do that in the back while I watched them for my entertainment, but I just drove around the clubs and bars. A man has to make his life enjoyable somehow. I never touched any of my passengers; I just gazed at them every time I had the chance. You can't blame a man for just ogling at someone's breasts can you? After all, it's my damn car you are traveling in!

Every night was quite the same, picking up passengers and dropping them wherever they wanted, but this night felt special. It was a dark, unusual night. No moon to be found in the night sky and surprisingly, just a single star. I wasn't bothered by the environment. too much. I just wanted to get done so I could go and buy more drinks for myself. It was 2:34 A.M. according to my watch and I was already feeling tired. There was an agonizing pain in my head which I ignored. I was driving around a Bar cum club in the very south of the city and as expected, I spotted a young couple trying to hail a cab from my right peripheral. "Oh Lucky day," I whispered after noticing the girl's exceptionally above-average features.

"I thought you won't come with me", said the boy to the girl as he opened the door for her. "But I am so glad you did darling."

"If I didn't I would have killed myself", she said with a smile, "Not missing a true gentleman."

'A true gentleman says to the lady, oh why are they so dumb', I thought to myself.

"You don't have to kill yourself love, please", said the boy amusingly.

"You still haven't told me where your place is," said the girl with excitement, "Still wanna keep it a surprise?"

"You'll see soon enough darling-- it'll be worth it," The boy told her, "Plus the place, you would find super hot."

"Oh, Baby can't wait!", The girl exclaimed.

"Take the southern bridge; take a right through the woods and you will see a mansion right after around two kilometers," informed the boy.

Without uttering a word, I started the car on our way. I drove for about twenty minutes and every time I peeked at them, I saw them getting closer and closer to each other, the boy had his arm around her shoulders and the other hand was gradually making its way to her thighs. We arrived at the bridge which was decently long and stretched for three kilometers. Straight roads are a blessing for me as I get more time to gawk at the back seat. Each second, the boy moved further tracing his hands on the surface of her skin. I felt the girl beginning to feel comfortable and just letting him take control. At this point, I was much immersed in it and the road seemed to have faded out for me, my hand tightly gripping the steering wheel and the other resting on my crotch. I finally noticed that the bridge had ended and I had to take a right, which I responsibly did. And my eyes right back ogling through the looking glass. I watched them go all out without a care in the world. I heard noises that blessed my ears. I was thoroughly enjoying the scenes that I was witnessing, the palm of my hands pressed to my crotch. I was about one and a half kilometers into the woods and there was still no sign of a mansion anywhere. Neither a proper path nor lights. Just pine trees everywhere. The action slowed down as the boy moved back from the girl who kept her eyes closed, wanting more.

"I have something for you darling", whispered the boy, but loud enough for me to hear.

The boy reached into his blazer's pocket, took out a dagger and buried it deep inside the base of the girl's neck, right in between the two collar bones.

I was terror-struck, my eyes popping out of their socket and my mouth open; I couldn't breathe.

The girl tried to scream but couldn't; the dagger was far down which prevented the scream. The boy started to chant something in a language that I wasn't familiar with. I had no idea what to do. 'Should I keep driving?', 'Should I stop?','What the hell do I do?'

The boy then violently took out the dagger from the girl's neck which resulted in a fountain of blood that shot out in multiple directions. The girl clutched her neck with her left hand and with her right slightly touching his face in disbelief. The girl blinked once before looking at the boy for the last time before closing her eyes forever.

"RIGHT HERE!" screamed the boy, "We would like to get off right here."

I stopped the car jerkingly, both hands gripping the steering wheel firmly and my eyes right in front. The boy pushed the girl's body outside, it fell with a thud. He chucked stacks of cash at me and said "You saw nothing". I nodded my head without looking at him. After he turned, using my peripherals I saw him drag the girl's body away. I stayed in the car silently without moving a muscle. 'Don't do it, just don't do it, drive off… JUST DO IT!' I exited the car and followed where the boy went. I walked for two to three minutes and started to see fire and people chanting perhaps the same language the boy was uttering back when he stabbed the girl with the dagger. All of them gathered around the fire with the girl right beside it. I tried not to make a sound but cursed luck! The leaves beneath my feet were dry. They all abruptly turned their heads, and looked at me all. My steps began to recede quickly and I fell back hitting my head on a hard surface.

I opened my eyes. It was a hospital ward. I was confused, disoriented, and unclear about the obscurity of the things I saw. Obviously, no one believed me when I told them the story; they said I hit my head quite well. A day later I was released from the hospital, they said my car was in the parking lot. I closely examined the car to find some proof of what I observed. There was nothing to be found. Giving up hope I sat in the car, turned the key and placed my foot on the brake pedal. I felt something odd about it. Upon close inspection, I found a stack of money smudged with bloody hand prints. I gazed at it for a few minutes straight before exchanging it for three bottles of vodka and a bottle of whisky.

~Alcoholism

Till I find you

The bells chimed as the doors swung open. Elijah came through the door drenched from the rain. He took off his coat and hung it on the coat holder by the door. "This is a nice café", whispered Elijah to himself.

"Welcome, sir. How can I help you today?" asked Derek, the bartender.

"An iced Americano please," said Elijah, placing himself on a high seat at the bar. "Not a lot of people here."

"Well, yes. Not a lot of people come through here, in fact, you are the fifth customer today."

"Fifth eh? All day?"

"Yes sir... all day... probably the final one for tonight"

"That's a shame, this place is quite cozy. Also, do you guys have wifi?" said Elijah, pressing on the wifi signal and turning it on, "My network sucks."

"We did have wifi when we first opened but due to budget cuts we shut it down," explained Derek as he started to make the iced Americano.

"Oh...Why do you think this place doesn't work?" Elijah curiously asked.

"I think it's because we have a weird concept. We have a bar but we don't serve alcohol, we serve tea and coffee. It's a strange blend of a café and a bar. Bar because we have this bar counter but no hard drinks and café because obviously, tea, coffee, and cakes."

"That sure is a strange combination..." Elijah said, putting his phone on the counter.

"Anyways sir what brings you here?" inquired Derek

"Umm..."

Derek looked at Elijah and saw tears forming in Elijah's eyes. "It's okay if you don't want to tell me"

Elijah looked up to Derek and smiled, "Don't call me 'sir'; its Elijah, just call me Elijah...it's been a long time since I told someone about this quest of mine."

"Only if you are okay with it...Elijah"

"It's about a woman...I lost her...years ago," said Elijah softly.

"I met her at my university...we were in the same class. She was... a friend of mine way before we physically met."

Elijah checked the time on his phone. 11:18 P.M.

"We were in fact best friends. Everything I did...I told her...everything she did... she told me..."

'Another generic unfulfilled love story,' crossed Derek's mind

"We soon became inseparable...Two creatures whose world revolved around each other. I fell in love...then she did...and hence began the journey of a lifetime...A lifetime..."

Derek passed the coffee that he had prepared while listening to Elijah.

"Thank you."

"I didn't feel complete the days I didn't see her. I was incomplete like this mobile device without the internet. She was my internet Derek, for my phone quite literally as well."

"We went to book fairs, bought no books. Cafes, she would have liked this café. Restaurants, amusement parks, libraries, circuses, markets, festivals, movies... gaming conventions, churches, museums, and a thousand other places, till every part of THAT city, reminded me...of her."

Derek sat down, threw a towel on his shoulder, and asked, "Then what happened?"

"Exploring the city took us to a range of different places, and one day...we ventured to a place where we shouldn't have."

Derek's interest grew and he listened with the utmost attention.

"We went on a drive, a long one, late at night. We usually stop in random places to 'explore' but we shouldn't have. This was outside the city—north-- there were ruins of an old fort, about two kilometers offroad by the highway. Like two reckless beings in their early twenties, we wandered off with our phone flashlights. Laughing, kissing, and singing we roamed and traversed into the woods. She mentioned how horrifying the pine trees looked. And it was true. After a while, she was creeped out by the darkness and the spookiness of the woods. She suggested that we turn back. But...I didn't listen... I encouraged her and persuaded her to walk further with me. She kept on telling me that she wasn't feeling good and she wanted to get out but I was stubborn...I dragged her with me..."

Derek got visibly uncomfortable. Elijah sipped on his drink and continued:

"Then we saw light, a fire in the distance and we heard a chanting noise. It was a different language. I felt the need to turn from there at that moment, but I turned to find a black figure standing at a distance. I screamed and rushed to ward off the light. I held her hand tight...We reached the fire to discover a group of people circled it and a girl's body lay beside it."

"A cult?", interrupted Derek. I have heard a story of a cult before, my sister told it to me— she is a nurse at the local hospital, she claims that a mad patient told her the story."

· "I don't know if it was a cult but the next thing I feel is a blow to my head and pictures of them taking her away from me...they took my Amy away" sobbed Elijah

Elijah's phone dinged multiple times as notifications poured in.

Derek passed a couple of napkins and sat beside Elijah. He placed his hand on Elijah's back and said, "There there, that is a crazy story."

"You don't believe me do you?"

"I do."

Elijah's phone dinged again.

"It was my fault, I took her there, it was my fault I forced her...I should have listened to her...How can I be so irresponsible?"

"You were young Elijah. I wouldn't blame you" said Derek trying to comfort him.

Elijah took a picture out of his pocket and showed it to Derek. "That's her."

"Pretty eyes," said Derek softly.

Elijah chuckled and said, " I see the whole universe in those eyes.

Elijah dabbed his eyes with the napkin and said, "I survived,-- I found myself in a dumpster in a different state with agonizing pain at the back of my head. I tried contacting her family back in her home town but they hadn't heard from her. No one has, I have no leads. And since then I have been trying to find her. I don't even know why I am here."

Elijah's phone dinged one last time before he picked it up to check. "Oh looks like your internet is working."

"That's not possible-- we don't even have a router anymore", said Derek confusingly.

Elijah pulled down the notification bar from the top, and his eyes popped out. It was connected to a network it hasn't been connected to for a very long time. It was getting weaker though. Elijah rushed out of the café keeping his eyes on the wifi signal. It got stronger, then dropped down. Elijah looked around him thoroughly, his eyes searching for someone. He looked back at his phone and noticed that the wifi signal had been lost. He knelt in the middle of a busy pedestrian way and gazed at the ground, defeated. Rain poured and thunder growled. ELIJAH caught a pair of feet stopping right in front of him. He traced the feet from his eyes all the way up to the person's face. A familiar face.

"Amy...I found you."

The raindrops seemed to have slowed down. Elijah's phone displayed a portrait of Amy and on top a strong signal of Wifi.

Amy smiled down at Elijah and softly said, "You found me...again."

~Suspended disbelief

Morningstar

"Let me get that for you" uttered Damon to an old lady trying to get something from a top shelf she wasn't able to reach.

"Oh thank you, dear. That is very sweet of you" smiled the old lady.

Damon got the jar of peanut butter and handed it to the lady. The lady tried to take the jar from his hands but he didn't let go.Damon's eyes scanned her body from head to toe. She applied a bit of force but Damon did not budge.

"Can I have this now boy...?"

The lady looked at his eyes, which were dead set on her eyes. His face appeared angry, frustrated, and on the verge of a meltdown. The lady showed signs of fear and receded her steps. Damon's face relaxed, his anger turned into a smile and he said, "Here you go ma'am" handing her the jar. The lady took the jar, placed it in her shopping cart, and hustled away.

"Ah...too old" sighed Damon.

He took out his cell phone from his right pocket and dialed a friend.

"Hey there Shawn. What's up?"

"It's going great Damon" he spoke softly "She is totally into me, this is it, I am bringing her tonight."

"Now don't be cocky Shawn, don't be blinded by overconfidence. Focus until the work is done."

"You don't know me, Damon. I am built differently. I am not you."

Damon was the black sheep of the group. All his other friends picked up girls like picking flowers in a garden. His approach was different from others; he always tried to sweet talk the ladies which never worked. Sweet talk might work long-term but these people simply didn't have the time or the commitment to do so. Damon was unable to take any girl back with him and was looked down upon in his group.

'I hate this! Why aren't there any nice girls around?!' thought Damon.

Damon put his hands inside his jacket and began to walk, gazing at every girl that passed by him. He gawked at them from head to toe, he noticed their bodies, breasts, hair, thighs, legs, feet...everything. He tried to nod at a few of them but none of them showed any kind of interest. 'It's not my day, it's never my day. It's always Shawn or Walter or Nix. Why can't I do it?'

Damon entered a café where a person wearing a biker's helmet immediately captured his attention. He was serving coffee.

'Why is he wearing a damn helmet indoors, what kind of a waiter wears a helmet while working?'

Damon took a seat at a small table and waited for him to take his order.

"Hello sir, my name is Sherley and I will be your waiter today."

"Oh no... I have a strange request, can he take my order?" said Damon pointing at the helmet-wearing person.

"You want Jeremy to take your order?" questioned Sherley.

"Jeremy...yes."

Sherley informed Jeremy about the situation and he obliged.

"You asked for me, sir?"

"Yes, Jeremy am I right?" asked Damon.

"Yes sir indeed, I know I am the most interesting figure here in this room."

"You sure are Jeremy."

Damon then proceeded to place an order. He ordered a black coffee with extra sugar.

"My break starts in a few minutes. If you don't mind, I would like to join you and answer your questions. That way I will be free and not compromise my work hours."

"That sounds good Jeremy, I'll wait here for you."

Time passed by, and Damon drank half of his coffee when Jeremy joined him sitting on the chair opposite him.

"I know...the helmet, that's the first thing you would ask me" assumed Jeremy.

"Naturally."

"So you see I have a tumor in my head, cancer. Uncurable. The light burns my eyes, it hurts beyond control, my head wobbles and I fall. I was kicked out of my last job due to this reason. These people hired me and to deal with my problem I wear this helmet, so my head stays stable and this shade helps me a lot with the headache caused by so much light."

Damon sipped his coffee listening to Jeremy with full concentration.

"You wear this helmet all the time?"

"No, not at night. I have minimal problems at night."

"I am so sorry man," Damon said, placing his hand on Jeremy's shoulder.

"Nothing either of us can do about it" sighed Jeremy.

Damon looked at the time on his wrist watch; it was 8:49 P.M.

"Damn! Would you look at the time? It's late, I shall leave now Jeremy, and I hope you feel well and find peace."

"Thanks for your concern sir," said Jeremy clearing up the table, "I wish you never see these days."

Damon exited the café as his phone rang. He took it out of his pocket and answered.

"Yes, Shawn?"

"Damon red alert, I have good and bad news."

"Go on ahead, good first please."

"Okay, so the good news is, today is the night, Lucifer shines bright tonight, and no moon just as we predicted. It is perfect, if we don't do it today, it's gonna be really bad."

"Right, but we predicted it to be today so it is not much of a surprise," said Damon unenthusiastically, "What's the bad news?"

"Bad news is...I lost the girl."

"WHAT!" screamed Damon attracting the attention of a few pedestrians. He noticed people looking at him so he moved out of the way and entered a dark narrow alley. "How the hell did you lose her? I thought you said you had this in the bag."

"I did but that bitch had to put her hand inside my jacket's pocket!" exclaimed Shawn, "She found my gun and the knife, it is on you now Damon, bring a girl by hook or crook, Force her if you have to."

"Me? I have never been able to pull one."

"I know and that is why you have to do it. I can not. I have a new task now, provided to me by Nix. I have to do it or else you know what happens. The last guy disobeyed him and didn't live to tell the tale."

"Where is Walter or John? Why me?" Damon said with anxiety creeping up on him.

"It has to be you, Damon, don't question the ways...do what is told," Said Shawn before hanging up the call.

Damon, without wasting a moment, rushed to his house. He groomed himself, wore a sharp blazer, with an appealing fragrance and he put on an attractive smile. He couldn't even recognize himself in the mirror anymore.

'Alright time to hit the club but before that...'

He called Shawn. But his phone was answered by Taris.

"Hello Shawn."

"Not Shawn...Taris."

"Taris...my lord...Lucifer glows bright."

Taris fell silent and then slowly whispered "Indeed Damon."

"I will get a woman there before dawn my lord, I promise" Said Damon putting his hand on his chest, "Lucifer's wish is our command, is my command. I will fulfill this, even if it requires my life."

"It is not your life the morning star seeks child...it was a woman's" explained Taris, "Bring a woman and you will be spared, failing to do so...would prove brutal for us."

Taris hung up the call and Damon hustled out of the house. He spent his evening and night at the bar cum club and was able to sweet talk a woman into his charm.

Jeremy drove outside the same bar. He was a cab driver looking for potential passengers. He spots the couple from his right peripheral and lets them in. The events that followed are still unfathomable to him.

~Sacrifice

Folklore

(This serves as an epilogue for each story)

The Interview

PSYCHO ON THE HIGHWAY!

16th September 2030.

Businessman murders wife and son over family quarrels. Reports from the murderer's neighborhood note loud noises were leaking out of his apartment throughout the night. People have also reported having witnessed signs of domestic abuse, in the form of scars and fresh wounds on both the bodies of the wife and the murderer. The murder weapon seems to be a sledgehammer which was swung onto the wife's head that killed her immediately and the kid was violently choked to death. The murderer was caught sobbing near a café on the highway, with the trunk of his Morris Minor open, containing the corpses. He had an interview the very same day, and in fact, it was the interviewer who called the cops. The identity of the interviewer remains unknown.

Tooth Fairy

Sleep is divine,

Phenomenon that passes time,

In the darkness of the night

Who knows what lies behind,

Perhaps an evil lurking in the gloom,

Carrying a grin and a ticket to your tomb

Don't Go

*Mary to a guard at the Lyssa Assylum: She was a parasite...
I did love her, I even told her not to go. She just wouldn't listen to
me! I finally decided to make her 'GO'!*

The Whispering

Wayfarer walks into the night;

Mufflers, jacket, mittens, he has a cold to fight:

Whispers in his ears, something's not quite right,

Is it a ghost? A witch? Or someone rather bright.

Fiction

Mrs. Darla: Is anyone there?

*She shone her flashlight between the narrow alleyways of the
library. In the distance a naked man, his biceps torn, ankle
broken, teeth wreathed with blood, crouching to evade the light.*

*Mrs. Darla: *__whispers__* I could have sworn I saw someone.*

[Leaves]

White Mask

Hoyot: I think I should go back to her…back home.

He stood overlooking a pile of nude dead bodies of women. The basement reeked, yet there was no resentment from him.

I Do

In the darkness of the desert unknown
Years passed, she feels alone
Skulks into the depths and dunes mountainous
She forced and developed a pleasant countenance.

Chauffeur

Shopkeeper: "Why is your money stained with blood?"
Chauffeur: "I tried slitting my wrists, did them halfway, then realized that alcohol is what I can live for. Now. Three vodkas and a whiskey."
Shopkeeper: "Yo, that's messed up dude!"

Till I find you

Elijah whispers to himself: God, I know it's my job to pray, even if I am praying for the impossible. The impossible is merely a construct. I am gonna pray till I find her…till I find her.

Morningstar

Fallen angel, deeply misunderstood
God's favorite, banished from his neighborhood.
How dare he question?
Compromised his flawless impression.

Tales From the Futrue

Firefall

No one knew how it started, people had their conspiracy theories, they blamed god, and the atheists were speechless, although a few of them had theories of their own, not a single one of them had the absolute answer. It started five years ago when flames engulfed the whole world. I remember looking up at the sky during a scorching hot summer day and thinking, 'What can possibly be worse than this?' And God...well he answered.

The lands that warmed up to forty degrees Celsius now burn with a flame that won't stop blazing for years to come. It still falls. I remember how it happened; it was not very long ago. Five years may not seem like a very long time but in this hole, time is slower than a snail. Sometimes I think it happened yesterday, and the rest of the time it feels like an eternity has passed. It is quite an uncanny feeling, a mystery just like the circumstance up above. I hear it every night when I sleep, the screams, the agony, the horror. There were signs before it happened but I guess they were not clear enough. How could it be? It's impossible. That's what I thought, that is what everyone would have thought if they put their mind to it. But all of us would have been proven otherwise...because the impossible occurred. It caught us off guard, unexpected; no one would expect such a thing. It would sound like a movie back then but now...it is our reality, the actuality of the world we currently live in.

Fire fell from above in the year 2137. From thin air, it fell. It started slow, and naturally, people were confused. Obviously, they were scared, and terrified, thinking that it was a terrorist attack. But the speculation was buried when it fell again, in different parts of the world. It could be an imperious heist pulled by the most powerful terrorist organization the world has ever known or it could be a phenomenon none of us were familiar with. Or it could just plain and simple be an act of God. A God who was sick of our actions, a God who can no longer tolerate all the pain and sufferings, a God who was furious with us, a God who just wanted to kill us all and get it over with. Why shouldn't he do it? We haven't been kind, moral, ethical, or even good. Yes, there are good people in this nearly hopeless world but the numbers are weak, they are minuscule, and it dwindles every day. Years before the flame fell there was war. The casualties were countless, and the damage of the war was incredible. It was irreversible. Even the good that I did meant nothing. A thousand barbaric acts were performed meanwhile. The number of rapes and crimes, in general, were increased by a hundred and twenty-eight percent in the year 2135 and it surged, even more, the next year. The year that followed after that was when the flame fell. I was on the sixty-fifth floor of a skyscraper when I saw scarlet clouds forming in the sky. The news ranted about these fiery clouds for days but on that day it was straight out of a fantasy novel. It seemed the clouds were soaked in blood. And it was then the flame fell.

I looked down to the buildings below, the roofs ignited, blazing more by the second. I saw my fellow employees scream in terror.

"We have been attacked, is it the Germans again?" screamed one of the employees.

I began my descent from the skyscraper with only one thought in my mind. My family...My Olivia. The elevator dinged open and I rushed out. I saw people running around, it was chaos. The giant glass doors of the exit opened wide and I stepped out. Heat consumed me. It was incredibly hot out there and I couldn't even breathe. Smoke and ash entered my lungs and I coughed uncontrollably. I rushed back inside with several people. The people threw themselves on the ground, their skins peeling off along with their clothes. The expensive suits and outfits proved to be useless in this condition. They rolled on the ground screaming and shouting for help but in a panic struck situation it is every man for himself. This was no ordinary circumstance to be in. It was one mankind had never faced. I like to believe it is the wrath of god.

I think of it now and I realize how crazy I was. I thought it was a good idea to venture off into the

"Firefall" in my car. Back then I was still young and not a drop of wisdom in my blood. I grabbed my keys from the key stand and hustled my way towards the parking lot in the basement. I entered my car, turned on the engine, and drove up. I broke past the barrier, and went through the black smoke, and into the flame. I drove trying to dodge the falling embers and make my way to my house but no luck. The fire fell like rain. Rain... a phenomenon I long to observe, with water of course. It wasn't long till my car was scorched. The fire melted my roof and poured hot metal on my suit. My body spasmed and I drove my car into a lamppost. It sparked and poured a cluster of incandescent particles onto my car's bonnet. Luckily I had a shade on top so at least I was safe from the flaming rain. I exited my car with what felt like a fractured leg. I limped my way into the closest building to escape the heat.

I threw myself on the ground, got rid of my jacket, and gazed out at the falling flame. A wave of hot air blew past me and the embers of the flame soared to me before extinguishing on my shirt.

'I am a dead man' I thought.

Just when all hope was lost I felt a hand on my shoulder.

"Hey. Let's go!" exclaimed the mystery hand. "Snap out of it! It's time to go time!"

He picked me up to my feet and I followed him, my ears were numb. A high-pitched noise wrapped my head until I was pushed into this sewer system.

For five long years, I have been here. In these five years, I have discovered so much. The safe houses down here are great, the facilities they provide are amazing and they surprise me every time. How were we even prepared for something like this? Did they know something like this was going to happen? It is still a riddle for me and everyone down here. A riddle I would like to decipher one day. But that day is not today, and I don't think the day is close. The day would come after I find my Olivia. With every passing day, I lose just a bit of hope. I wish to find her before all my hope is lost. That is the only dream I see now, asleep or even awake.

~God's Wrath

Glory of the Same Summer Sun

This morning was supposed to be special; it was the day when I came to this world eighteen years ago. Great news for my family, or was it? I was an unwanted child, I realized that at the age of fourteen. My parents wanted a girl but surprise! It was me. "Kasper! Wake up I have planned an amazing day for you today" said my obnoxious brother. 'You are twenty-nine, unemployed, still living with us, for God's sake, just get out already.' Obviously, I didn't have the power to say that to his face because I don't want any more drama to bother me anymore.

"Lux, talk to me."

"Good morning master Kasper, and Happy Birthday, Let me calculate how many calories you would be requiring today. Meanwhile, let me tell you about the world," said the AI robot with enthusiasm.

"Here he goes" sighed Kasper.

"Yesterday there was an armed robbery just two miles away from here. Three people died, all due to the plasma rifles. I suggest you wear the shield emitter that your father bought you."

"Yeah whatever Lux, just tell me about the weather."

"The weather is a beautiful nineteen degrees Celsius with heavy rain expected around three o'clock."

"When the hell does it not rain?" I said to myself but audible enough for the AI to hear me.

"Well master Kasper the last time it didn't rain was on the 7th of March 2134, where the sun shone brightly providing a warm blanket of light. It was one day prior to your birth."

"Must have been beautiful day…"

Then they screwed the weather by sending all the gas missiles and other stupid things into the sky. It never stopped raining. The two years were difficult for the people but eventually, people lost hope and adapted to the gloomy condition.

"What is Mace?" I asked my brother. "Are you gonna spend more of dad's money today?"

My dad gave me a look through his transparent tablet in which he was reading the news.

"Get this, drum rolls; we are taking you to see the sun!" he says with sheer excitement.

"The Sun?"

"Yes the big giant ball of fire that disappeared just before you were born."

"It didn't disappear, dear, it's just hidden by the clouds that cover the sky," said our mother in the sweetest way possible.

Although I didn't like my family all that much, I was still a part of them and can't afford to live on my own just yet so I have to be careful with what I do or say.

"And how exactly are we going to see the sun?"

"Space travel, duh! Now we can't separate the clouds and see the sun, can we? It didn't work."

"That's great," I said in a sarcastic tone.

I was skeptical but very excited. I didn't want to be this hyped because everything I have had faith in or had expectations for had failed me terribly. It was time to keep them low so I could never be disappointed. But it was the Sun, it has been my lifelong dream to see the blazing ball in the sky, to feel its warm clutches to 'drink a cold beverage, under the hot summer sun.' This was probably the closest thing I could have to make that dream into reality and my heart refused to stay calm about it. I acted mature and even though I am well past the innocent child phase, come on; I was just eighteen years old. Why would I want to be an adult anyway? I think it was because of the unwanted attitude that I received as a kid that molded me in such a way.

We reached the place after three hours of traveling in the new hover car that dad bought Mace for his birthday. As we approached the structure I heard sounds and even saw space shuttles take off in the distance. My stomach was tickling and my grin was expanding. I was going to see the sun in a few minutes. In the waiting room, Mace and I went through various exercises that were the preparation for being in space. We got suited up and sat tightly.

"So... how excited are you?" asked Mace happily.

"I-I would like to thank you brother," I said with tears clogging my eyes "I know I haven't been the best brother, and have said you many things that you did not deserve to hear, I am sorry."

"Hey Hey Hey, it's okay Kasper, there is nothing to cry about," he said, embracing me. "All of us are different, each one of us. I know you don't love us and that's alright. You shouldn't choose whom you love cause that's not it... Love is an instinct that kicks in when you find it."

"Now, Now, let's not show the sun you're crying face. Cheer up buddy and let's go, our shuttle is ready."

The ship took off and I felt the acceleration push my body. A weird fume crept into the airlock which smelled awful, but I ignored that. Tears ran along my temples and my hand gripped my brother's hand. After a few minutes, we cut through the thick, never-ending clouds and exited the atmosphere. Some time passed and our safety straps clicked open and an automated voice said "The window shade will now open, please wear your UV protection glasses."

All of us gathered before the window waiting for it to open and it did. The shutters slowly began to rise. Saw the light shine on my legs to my hips and finally, I saw the sun in all its glory. Bright, shiny, warm, and all the other feelings my parents felt back in the day. The warm embrace of the burning sun; basking in its glory was the best thing I have ever felt. I turn my eyes to Mace, smiling at the sight. My mind flashed with the memory of yesterday night when I stood by his side while he slept peacefully. A knife in my hand and intent so barbaric even I contemplate it now. It is good that I didn't take that road. I am proud of myself. What would have happened if I went ahead with it? Well, it didn't happen so no need to think about it I guess. Or maybe I should think about it, what if it happens one day? Either way, it's not happening right now.

I match the same smile my brother carried and gazed back to the Sun, soaking the tenderness of the flaming celestial object floating in an unknown point of the vast endless universe.

~How much does it take to light up my thoughts?

Saudade

"Earth is finished. It is exploited beyond repair, we didn't control ourselves and now it is over, we are done for. There is no planet B, Damn it! We are all gonna die here."

A man on the news said these seventeen years ago in the year 2074. The world was a much better place back then, yes we were on the brink of collapse, yes we had almost exhausted all the resources our planet had to yield, but the planet had hope. Hope, that was supposed to be the people, but that hope started to fade with the introduction of the H.A.F.H (Home Away from Home) series of luxurious spacecrafts that can hold a million people.

After the world plunged into another world war in the year 2055, it was in shambles. Prior to the war, the world was multi-polar with multiple superpowers but after the war in 2059, it turned Uni-polar with the USA being the only superpower left. The massive casualties of the war dwindled the earth's population significantly. There were a lot fewer people on earth seventeen years ago and there are even fewer right now. Operation FNL (Finding a New Life) began in the year 2080 when they started sending people to space. The H.A.F.H took them to the nearest habitable Star system, it was quite similar to our solar system. Why didn't they dock all those ships in our solar system? The answer to that was "The further the better". A getaway. An escape. More like abandoning the place that they once called... "Home." Some elderly people said that this reminded them of a very old animated film that their parents made them watch as kids.

Hundreds if not thousands of HAFHs were manufactured by the efforts of almost every industry, company, enterprise, and individuals who wanted to just leave earth once and for all. Each is equipped with all the necessities human beings need to survive and lead a fruitful life. They wanted to jump out of the sinking ship but make another ship made out of the planks of the drowning one. And they succeeded. By the year 2088, after hundreds of HAFHs leaving earth, I was able to book a ticket for myself. Mine would take off in a few weeks from now and I am one of the last passengers to board the final remaining HAFH. My HAFH was delayed and delayed again due to severe weather conditions. There were clouds in the sky. There was something odd about it. Never in my life had I seen such conditions. They were dark, dense, and mysterious, almost like someone's eyes, I don't remember who but someone close to me. Someone I lost during the war. I was getting old and my memory was not as sharp as I thought it would be. Did I want to remember the dark times? Absolutely not. So I wasn't too bothered about my memory loss. But everything comes at a price and losing my memories would mean losing the last fragment of... her.

The clouds never poured rain. It just loomed and growled. With time the growling began to grow stronger and the days became darker. Every passing day seemed like the earth was moving further away from the sun. After months of delay, they decided to test the atmosphere for takeoff. They tested with multiple rockets and space shuttles and they were all struck down by lightning, none of them made it out of the outer atmosphere which induced panic among the people down here. A few days passed and the weather started to be graceful again, sun began to shine through the thick clouds and it seemed that takeoff would be possible. Without wasting any time they hoarded the people in the HAFH and prepared for takeoff. There were a few skeptical people who refused to board the ship and demanded to stay till the weather gets better. It was the last HAFH but it wasn't the last shuttle. Half a dozen shuttles would take off carrying the final traces of humanity from earth, at least that's what they thought. I was one of the skeptical ones and wanted to stay behind, not because I was scared to die in a crash but because I was afraid to leave earth forever. It was like something was stopping me from getting onto that HAFH and I had no idea what. So I delayed my departure and joined the people who were supposed to take the shuttle after a few days of the HAFH's departure.

I was there when it took off. The spacecraft was a structure that was equivalent to a thousand buildings. It was close to impossible to lift such a humongous structure off the ground and into outer space so they use a device that alters the gravitational pull of the earth for a limited amount of time which gives the HAFH the adequate support to lift off and enter space. I saw the megastructure lift off and soar into the sky and just when I thought it was gone, I saw clouds magically appear. With the same dark and raging clouds, it looked as if an iron wall had appeared. At once the HAFH was struck by lightning multiple times. It resisted the lightning bolts at first but then it hit something amongst the clouds, followed by another wave of thunder. Right before my eyes it came crashing down, chunks and pieces of the megastructure started to fall on earth. It was like an earthquake that we felt even though we were staying numerous kilometers away from the epicenter.

After the incident, the shuttles would still take us to the nearest HAFH out there, but the people were more scared than ever. Although they were willing to die in a crash to rather stay in this "Hell". I for one, ventured out in the wild to make some memories before I fly out in that shuttle and never see earth again. I may reach a HAFH or I might even die on my way. Either way, it is a good idea to get the feel of the earth one last time.

On my adventure, I expected to find wild mutated animals, insects, and various other kinds of weird things but to my surprise I found people. They were about a few hundred of them and had no intentions to leave earth. Upon Investigating further I found out that it was a cult of people who still have hope that they can turn around the situation and make this planet habitable again. In the middle of them all I saw a lady, 'The oracle' who kept on chanting "She doesn't want us to go, she is sad, she'll be lonely". I spent time with these people and the more I did that, the more I was convinced to stay. And eventually, I did stay. They turned around the state of the planet, obviously not entirely but just enough to survive. It was a small closed society that protected each other, and at times of crisis helped each other.

Ten years passed.

"Uncle Richy, can you tell us about the time Mother Earth didn't let the last HAFH fly away?" asked a curious little boy.

"What? HAFH? What are you talking about?" I was thoroughly confused.

"Leave old man Richy alone, he doesn't remember anything," said a woman from a distance.

"Richy... is that my name? I suppose it is."

I find it hard to remember my name nowadays, in fact, it's hard to remember anything. All I have are blurry faded visions of the past. A pair of eyes standing out from the crowd, I remember them clearly. Dark, dense, and mystical. It's almost like I am still lost in them.

~Alzheimer

Cavern of the Lost Souls

The world has advanced. It has evolved from the wreck and people live in harmony. They colonized Mars in the year 2042, broke new grounds in space exploration, and have even sent satellites to "Andromeda". There was a point when the earthlings became so immersed and occupied with space travel they skipped the fact that they haven't even fully explored their own world yet. The vast oceans remained unexplored. Two years ago in the year 2049, they realized their ignorance and hence started "Probing Mother Earth". A drive mission with the aim to extensively explore their home planet.

Jackson, a twenty-five-year-old explorer, was assigned a certain part of Antarctica. He was hoping that he would get to the depths of the pacific ocean but unfortunately for him, he received the bone-chilling climate of Antarctica.

"Antony, you lucky bastard, have fun scouting the waters of the Indian Ocean", said Jackson waving goodbye to him, "Make sure Varun doesn't drown."

"Don't worry about that Jacky, I will have fun, that's for sure, only if a sea monster doesn't eat me" responded Antony, "Tell you what, I'll bring you a fish."

Antony winked at Jackson as he got on the bus with the rest of his crew. The bus door closed and was on its way to the airport.

Jackson really wanted to explore the oceans. He was a Thalassophile. He didn't particularly hate the freezing atmosphere of Antarctica but he didn't prefer to be there either.

Jackson, along with his team of three other explorers was to investigate a cavern that was infamous for not letting explorers out. It is exceptionally dark there and reports of never before seen beasts are rumored around. A group of explorers went inside the cavern in the year 2025, back when it was discovered, but there was something odd about it. The communication was hindered by some sort of blocker. No one knew if it was natural, or manmade. The team of five young and strong survivalists wandered inside, but none came back. A few weeks later a search party was sent to extract them. The search party consisted of eight people and just like the previous company, none came back. The cavern was dubbed the "Cavern of the lost souls". No modern equipment seemed to work around or inside the cavern. It was like using electric equipment near reactor number four in Chornobyl in 1986. Drones dropped from midair, rovers died immediately after entering, mobiles, walkie-talkies, nothing worked. They checked for radiation but still found nothing at all. A few years later in 2035 a set of brave soldiers showed the courage to go inside. There were a dozen of them, brave, brawny, and smart. They took with them equipment which could withstand a drop from the empire state building and had the power to resist any sort of blocking device. The team stationed outside the cavern was super confident and thought that this was going to be a cakewalk. But there was a lingering doubt in everybody's mind, 'What if it doesn't?" The communication signals were strong and the army of men marched down deeper into the icy cavern.

"It's incredibly dark down here", said team leader Blake.

"I hate the dark, I only signed up for this, so I can shoot some aliens or monsters or whatever lies here," said the most muscular one of the group, "All I find here is darkness."

"It's Dark like your mother's room last night sergeant," said Blake.

The team shared a good laugh, except for the muscular guy.

"I'll let it slide now, Commander..." he said, not amused.

The signal buffered as they kept going deeper inside the cavern.

"I see something, I see, HaHa, I see light" Blake screamed.

Blake saw a blue gleaming glow in the distance and he rushed towards it. It was a tunnel made up of solid ice. Sunlight shone on the surface which resulted in the tunnel beaming so much light.

"This place is majestic" uttered a soldier dropping his jaw.

The signal was buffering even more.

"Can yo- still hea- us Com...der -ake?" said the voice on the radio.

"Barely, but it's still good. I was thin-"

Blake saw something move at the very end of the tunnel.

"Boys, I think I found your monster, let's get it!"

The men rushed to satisfy their curiosity.

"Don't mak-quic- decisions, think -ake" stammered the radio.

Outside the cavern a group of scientists and expedition managers were assembled in the tent, listening and managing the mission. The last thing they heard through the communication system was:

"Is that a human? It can't be...he is gray...huge...wait what is it... Holy mother of god...RETREAT! Run boys... HOW? How is this even possible...there is NO way...I thought my grandfather killed the last of you! Need back up, need back up! Oh my... OH MY GOD!"

The radio uttered nothing but static noise after that. The last thing their camera was able to transmit was a blur of giant gray figures in the distance. A beast? A machine? A human? No one knows.

A few hours passed by and when it seemed that all the hopes had died, out came Commander Blake, running and half naked. His uniform burned away, and his skin with major third-degree burns. He held a red and white torn piece of fabric in his hand.

"They are back...oh no no, they never left," he said before having a cardiac arrest. He died a day later.

Jackson was assigned the same cavern. The "Cavern of the lost souls". He wasn't scared, advanced machinery by his side, and he felt confident as ever. They had custom-made suits, and even gravity-defying gadgets. They had plasma weapons and boots and gloves that could stick to any surface. The situation was great equipment-wise. The morale was high and there was no stopping them.

Jackson and his team tread their way into the cavern with minimal fear thanks to all the gadgets and equipment. Danny, another friend of Jackson, was one of the team members. They came across the same brightly lit ice tunnel and communication signals were strong as ever. They had their chest high up and showed no hesitation. They crossed obstacles and were going on strong...until, all of a sudden the equipment gave up. The boots, the gloves, and the suits all lost their effect. The suits were self-warming and now that they had stopped working Jackson and the company felt cold. Panic struck and one of them suggested that they should turn back. But Jackson insisted they keep moving. It was dark again. The camera on their head streamed the video outside to the researchers. But it was short-lived the camera connection got disconnected as well as they went deeper inside the cavern. Yet again there was just static for the outside people.

"I think we have lost comms," said Jackson pressing his ear.

Jackson turns to his comrades and sees a sight that sends a shock down his spine. One of his colleagues is down on the ground in a pool of his own blood. And the other two were incapacitated by a giant gray beast. Jackson shot his Plasma rifle at the mysterious figure and the shot bounced off of him and landed on Danny's head. He instantly died, the plasma bullets were no joke they had the power to take down trucks. The massive figure approached Jackson.

Jackson looked closely and confusingly said, "A...machine?"

He was then struck on his head which put him unconscious.

Jackson struggled to open his eyes, his vision blurred. He was being dragged by the 'Machine'. It chucked Jackson's body in the middle of an enclosed area that resembled some sort of throne room. From the cloudy vision, Jackson did spot a throne. He saw someone sitting on it but couldn't make out his features. Around him everything was modern. Jackson contemplated whether he was in a cavern in Antarctica or a building in New York. He saw people, uncountable, like a small city down here. All of them were wearing uniforms. Jackson, still with his foggy sight, notices something similar in all their uniforms. They all had a red band around their left arm.

"It can not be…" whispered Jackson turning his face to the throne, his vision clearing up.

He saw a person sitting on the throne, his limbs made of machines, half his head was a machine, and even his torso had visible organs made up of machines. A cyborg, a mix of human and machine, he had no hair but gray strings of thread styled in a very recognizable way. And just below his nose, a toothbrush mustache.

"Heil Hitler!" shouted everyone around Jackson raising their arms for the Nazi salute.

It was Adolf Hitler that sat on the throne looking down on Jackson.

"Führer, I brought you new entertainment"

"But…how…?" sighed Jackson with disbelief.

"Technology…Technology had kept me…alive" said an automated voice from a speaker attached to Hitler's throat.

"I faked my death all those years ago. I gathered my followers, scientists, engineers, and whoever supported me and we arrived…here. A huge meteor struck this part of Antarctica centuries ago and it was the most advanced thing anyone had ever seen. We learned how to harness its power and look at us now. We Nazis are the most advanced civilization there is. I am waiting… for more of humanity to shift to Mars, so we can strike again. I have built my army and we are ready. This time we strike hard... with the power of the meteor, no one... can stop us. You must be wondering why I am telling you all this. Well. You are the final visitor here before we strike. I have waited enough. We wreak havoc. WE Destroy!"

He rose after delivering the final sentence and the crowd went wild. They chanted his name, saluted him, and kissed the swastika on their arms.

Jackson was stripped from all his weapons but one. The 'cyanide' of the current time. There was no question, he had to do it. He stood up at once and ran towards him. He dodged a guard and hugged Hitler.

"What are you doing?" He tried to push Jackson away.

"You like technology?" he said with rage, "This is called a 'Plasma imploder.'"

Jackson bit into a tooth he set loose inside his mouth and like a black hole, force and pressure converged at one point in his mouth before exploding Jackson's face. He caught Hitler in the blast radius, blowing him away.

"Führer!" screamed a bunch of concerned followers.

They go to check on him just to find him dead. His brain is in pieces and an exposed skull, half human, half machine. The whole colony mourned the death of their leader, they killed themselves due to the loss of hope, the loss of the only person they lived for. Their half-mechanical bodies were not affected but the human parts froze after death.

Ten years later another expedition arrived and discovered the secrets of the place. They found hundreds if not thousands of dead Nazis. It became a sensation on the news and researchers are still trying to comprehend the events that took place there for decades.

~Look he's alive! Nevermind...he's dead.

Astral Home

A myriad of people began to live in my home city of 'Warqet' when the neighboring country fell under the long oppression of the British. It was the year 2188, they finally took over and the people were scattered everywhere. The people will never learn, wars, fights, and conflicts will be a part of us as long as we live and breathe. Although the advancement of technology was not hindered by all this drama. It only became more advanced the next day you woke up. Overpopulation was a major problem, especially in the city I lived in. One fine day I woke up to find millions of people requiring shelter and food to survive. I was in my early twenties back then, I was selfish and I refused to give up anything of my own to the people who needed it more than me. Eventually, I did open my heart and began to help and volunteer, but the years have not done that, hits me to this day. The roads are still filled to the brim with people everywhere, tents, hammocks, mattresses, and other things required to survive. I do not remember when was the last time I saw the city without smog. The city had a post-apocalyptic feel as if we had survived a nuke and this is how we lived now. Graffiti on the wall, fires, and the unending snowfalls nine months a year. The citizens who already had a house were the luckiest bunch. I was one of them, Thanks to my father who left the apartment under my name. Surprisingly the chaos didn't affect my academics; I achieved great heights and am currently working on the 'Astral Home' project. I work at the looming tower above the clouds where we are determined to find these 'wanderers' a place to call home. We had an incredible breakthrough last month, we found plenty of alternate dimensions. Tests have been concluded and tomorrow, I along with a small team of researchers will venture inside for human exposure testing. It is said that the environment is safe and perfectly habitable for human life.

Today is the day. The day we make history, the first humans that we know of to enter an alternate dimension. I ride my bike to work daily and today was no different. It wasn't like I couldn't afford a car but the streets of Warqet were no less than slums. The bike was the most convenient option. I wear my helmet, lock the door behind me and leave. Paddling through the topsy-turvy way, out to the main road were on the sides were families around fires drinking soup. I see children playing with hoverboards and their parents watching them over using their bionic eyes. Neon holograms floated near buildings that collected algae and had a thin coat of snow. Smoke and fog swished and wrapped me as I gradually cut through the mist. The light of the headlight was almost folly, it merely illuminated a few feet of the path ahead of me. I emerged out of the crowded neighborhood, onto a wide straight road that led directly to my workplace. In the distance among the white-washed landscape stood a tall tower, dubbed "The Looming Tower of Doom". People call it that because they think we experiment on humans there. It's stupid, we work our asses off to find these people a new home and that's how they show their gratitude. I was overjoyed to hear about the discovery of the dimensions, at least there won't be people chilling on every road. The tower was so tall that the top of the tower was rarely visible from the ground, except that one day when we had a clear sky and the rectangle top floor of the looming tower shone brightly like an alien presence. They feared it, some even considered an uninvited visit, but thankfully nothing was executed.

I reached the base of the tower and got heavily judged by a handful of protesters outside the gate as I scanned my biometrics to get into the building.

"Good Morning Henry", said the security robot

I got into the elevator and pressed the button which had '201' printed on it.

I found many things in my great-grandfather's storage house, one of which was a book called "Charlie and the Chocolate Factory". It was a great read. This elevator always reminded me of the one in that story. I oversaw floor after floor, each bustling with its workers till I reached my floor. 201. The elevator dinged open.

"Henry!" screamed a group all at once, one louder than the others

"Yes yes guys, I am here", I said with a smug "Always the loudest eh Neil"

"Hell yeah!" screamed Neil with overflowing enthusiasm, "Everything is set, just ready up and we are good to go"

"On it", I imitated finger guns at Neil before I went inside the locker room.

I suited up and after a few test scans, all of us stood in the airlock waiting for them to open the first portal.

Samantha, the head of the project appeared on a screen before us.

"Brave men. That's what you are. Risking your welfare in search of a new home for millions of people. You people deserve the highest honor."

I have always admired Samantha for her confidence and ability to stand her ground no matter what. She was rejected multiple times by the government to fund this project but she somehow got billionaires involved and very smartly set the whole charade up. The government had no other choice but to oblige.

"From the intel that I have received from a month-long observation and research of these alternate dimensions, I have a few instructions that you have to strictly follow. Failure in abiding by these would prove fatal to the space-time continuum. I will only say it once, so listen close. There are... let's call it, different kinds of presence we have felt in the various dimensions that we have discovered. It seems like it's something supernatural, but don't you stress. We have found out that it is harmless. But we still advise extreme caution. You never know what wants to come here with you. Now, some straight notes. If you see a dark humanoid figure in the distance, DO NOT look at it in the eyes. Even if it comes very close to you. Ignore it and just keep walking. If you see a house that looks way too familiar to you, DO NOT enter it, you may never return. If you hear someone calling for you, perhaps and most possibly an attractive figure, DO NOT heed attention. There would be artifacts that look like gold, diamonds, and whatever attracts you, DO NOT pick them up. A garden filled with vibrant trees, flowers, and fruit, DO NOT eat any of it. If you feel cold, extreme cold... I want you to get away from that area as soon as possible, that's something you cannot touch, but it can touch you... and lastly, if you see a black dot in the distance, turn, and run back here as fast as you can."

The grin on my face faded as she went on and when she finished speaking I looked at my team expecting the same reaction as me but I was utterly shocked. Their smiles grew and they were pumped to step out of the portal as soon as it would open.

"There are a lot of different anomalies that we might have not discovered yet so just be careful. With all that being said, Good luck!" she said before the screen retracted.

"Guys! How can you be so ignorant!?" I exclaimed, "It's clearly not safe for us to go out there"

Neil turned around and said "Getting cold feet now Henry?"

"My whole body is cold damn it! This is not safe yet!"

'Warning, portal opening in 5'

"This is crazy" Henry whispered

'4'

Henry clenched his fists.

'3'

He closed his eyes shut tightly.

'2'

"Please God, help us"

'1'

Henry was expecting a creature or some force to pounce on them and rip their throats off.

'Zero'

A whooshing noise covered the room. The air began to rush at the spot, blue particles sparked like thunder, the glass on Neil's helmet reflected the spectacle, and his eyes wide open with optimism. The ground began to shake, the blue particles started to accumulate in one particular spot before expanding. As the portal became larger by the second they were able to see what was on the other side. It was green, it looked like grass. A high-pitched noise pierced through their ears before the portal finally opened. A circular door floating in mid-air. A doorway to a world or perhaps a universe unexplored by mankind.

"Breakthrough!" screamed Neil.

Henry felt a quiet calm, following the chaos. He slowly opened his eyes. Bright light from the portal was almost blinding. His eyes adjusted and he got closer to have a better look. The image through the portal was blurry; it was like looking at the world with thick dirty glass.

'Portal to World 1 a.k.a. "The Swamp" is now open. Please step inside the portal.

"Let's go boys" Neil led the group, "And Henry if you don't wanna come that's fine too, you can just go back and help the Janitor."

The group chuckled and turned their faces away and towards the portal. Henry thought it is not actually a bad idea to back off, but he has been waiting his whole life for this moment. Every decision, choice, consequence, and path has led him to this moment. It was too late to back out and his ego just won't let that happen anyway. 'How bad can it be...?' he whispered under his breath and stepped into the portal with the rest of the team. The light shone bright, there was no actual source of the light, like our sun, the sky simply beamed with the color green. Henry looked at the 'grass' below his feet as he brushed his boots on the surface. "Amazing."

The team scattered, each trying to satisfy their own set of curiosities about the place. It was like they were kids who just entered a chocolate factory where everything was made of chocolates.

"There is so much green here" Whispered Henry to himself.

Green hasn't been Henry's favorite color, he has always been a red person. The color of a fresh apple, a rose, his wife's lipstick, the color of blood...color of danger. He walked slowly and steadily, the gravity of this place was less effective, it was said that it was 5 times lower than it is on earth. But the special suits were well equipped for situations like these. The suits kept their bodies and feet stuck to the ground.

"This is not it guys, sure this place seems fine for a living but all this green will just not be tolerable" suggested Li, their crewmate.

"I agree" replied Neil, "Now that we are here, we shall just explore this place a bit."

"Hell yeah" Chanted Jonsey.

"Why is the place called 'The Swamp' again?" enquired Henry.

"I'll show you..." Neil uttered softly, "Everybody to my position."

Ten brave men stood before two enormous cave entrances. The two entrances were split by a soft wall, also the same material that made the ground. The whole structure looked like a triangle, with two caves on two sides and a wall in between splitting them apart. The men felt the wind behaving abnormally. The cold wind went inside and a second later warm air exited and breezed past them. "Before we leave this world, let's check this out," Neil said with confidence. The team headed inside turning on the light on their helmets. The surface of the cave was sticky and as expected, gloomy green. Long strands of thick dark green rocks covered in what looked like algae. "I can feel the wretched smell creep in my suit," said Ronald.

"Let's just get a sample and get out of here," Henry said.

Neil set down the briefcase on the ground and took out a 'probing drill'. "This little fella can drill deep down collect the samples that we need and come right back up to us." He turned a few knobs and pressed a button. He set the machine on the ground and a few seconds later it began to drill. "There it goes."

As soon as the drill penetrated the surface, a gloop of green liquid began to emerge from inside. "Ew, what's this?!" Henry, perplexed.

"We don't know, that's why we are here taking sample dummy" laughed Jonsey. A few seconds later abruptly the ground shook. The to-and-fro wind became quicker. The pattern of the wind was identical to breathing. It was low and calm before, but right after the 'Probing Drill' it fastened. The wind became so strong that it blew them away and then pulled them inside. Their bodies were rag-dolling inside the cave.

"Get out of here!" screamed Neil.

"That's what we are trying to do" replied Henry "Use your jet packs, FLY YOU FOOLS!" The team uses their Jet packs to fly out of the cave. They see the surface move. They raced toward the portal in the distance which looked like it was flickering.

"This... is not grass... it's fur...," Henry said slowly, his voice giving the rest of the team goosebumps. One by one they flew through the portal and crashed into the room destroying some equipment and majorly denting the walls. The portal shrunk in itself before closing.

"WHAT THE HELL WAS THAT?" screamed Neil.

The probe drill, which he somehow managed to retrieve, in an automated voice said, "Analysis: Living organism. Species: Unknown. Origin: Astral-97 (A-97)."

"That was crazy, we were on a living thing?" stammered Li

"From what I think, we were inside its nose..." Henry answered.

The expedition leader once again appeared on a screen before them.

"So it looks like the first potential world was a failure."

"World?" shouted Henry "In what universe do you think that it was a world? It was an organism, a living one! We just walked into its nose!"

"I am aware of the circumstances Mr. Henry and don't you dare raise your voice with me. So now, we shall explore the three remaining potential worlds."

"You crazy bitch! We are not going back in there" said Ronald standing up, "Get me out of here, I QUIT!"

"That's a shame Mr. Ronald" she smiled, "Can we please get Mr. Ronald the exit please, his suit number is..."

"Number 7" interrupted Ronald.

"Yes...suit number 7. Thank You."

The lights changed color. The brightly lit white room was now a bloody red. Ronald's suit made a noise and it began to compress.

"Wait what's happening?" said Ronald confusingly.

His body ached, limbs jammed, neck choked. He couldn't breathe, and his suit became tighter by the second. Ronald screamed in agony as his bones cracked. His skin tore due to the compression, and his body shrunk. Leaving his head, every part of his body was under an insane amount of pressure. Blood clogged his eyes and then poured out. His organs squashed and mashed, his bones shattered into a million pieces. The team was horrified to witness a sight before them, all of them sticking their back to the walls gawking with disbelief. Ronald's body lay flat on the ground with a couple of liters of blood inside his helmet.

"Consider that a warning..." said Samantha menacingly, followed by a smile, "Now the rest of you, nine, let's get this done, shall we? Open the second portal and escort Mr. Ronald out"

A pair of armored soldiers entered the airlock and carried the body out. The team shared eye contact but none of them uttered a single word.

"Take your positions," said a recorded automated voice. "Good Luck"

The remaining nine took their positions, silent as ever, and patiently waited for the portal to open. Neil and Henry made eye contact and Neil could read the look on his face, screaming 'I told you so'. The same blue particles collided in one place. Like thunder indoors the portal opened. The blurred picture this time was darkness. No other color except absolute black.

"A-485 is now open"

"Here goes nothing," said Henry before making contact with the blur using his fingers. His fingers enter the world before his whole body phases through. The team was inside, they looked around and found nothing but darkness. Yet they could see each other clear as day.

"How is this happening? It's so dark here, we shouldn't be able to see each other, How?" asked Jonsey confused.

"What's this liquid beneath our feet?" Neil said softly "It's gooey and slimy, ew"

"It's kinda like oil," said Desmond tip tapping his feet

"Alright boys, split into teams of three, each goes in different directions and meets back at the portal after twenty minutes of exploring," said Neil setting a timer on his watch which he wore over the suit.

They split into teams of three and commenced their exploration.

"This place gives me the chills" whispered Henry to himself.

"Yeah this place sucks" replied Desmond.

"Anyway guys, I don't think there is much to this place, it's all just black and dark and this oily substance is getting to me."

"Yeah...but let us just check that house over there," said Desmond.

"A house? Where?" said Henry erecting his arms to the side, "You sure you okay Desmond?

Desmond pointed his finger past Henry's right arm and said "Right over there...clear as day"

Herny turned and saw nothing. "What are you talking about?"

"I am going to investigate" Desmond began to walk towards a freshly red-painted two-story high house with a sturdy wooden door with two pillars in front.

The step he took was not reluctant, rather they were heading towards a fixed destination. Henry tried to stop him but Desmond showed no signs of slowing down.

"Henry, it is my Grand ma's house"

"Desmond stop! Don't you remember what Samantha said?" Henry quickened his pace, "Don't go into a building that looks familiar!"

"You don't know Henry! I lost my grandma when I was ten, ravaged by the 'survivors' on the streets of our town! I wanna see her!" he sprinted toward the house's entrance.

"Josh helped him stop him!" Henry screamed looking back. He saw Josh staring into the distance with his arm dangling beside him. He was following Henry moments ago and now he stood there clueless. His mouth appeared to be drooling and his eyes were half closed.

"Oh no Josh" he turned away from him and double-timed behind Desmond. Right before he could tackle him, Desmond used his jet pack to fly and approached the house at terminal velocity.

"Grandma..." is what Henry heard come through his earpiece before Josh slammed into the house, breaking the wooden door and along with it his neck and spine. To Henry's eyes, it looked like Desmond collided with thin air and fell flat in the black oil substance.

"Desmond!"

He jet-packed towards him but while he was hovering in the air, he saw the black 'gloop' wrap around Desmond's lifeless body and swallow it. Henry landed where the body lay and there was nothing there. No signs of any house or Desmond. The gloop beside his feet wobbled as if it was alive.

"I need to get back to Josh."

He used his Jet pack yet again to fly towards Josh, but as he took off, a string of gloop emerged from the ground and caught his leg. "What?!" Panic struck, Henry tried to boost his jet pack and use the remaining fuel to get rid of the gloop and it almost worked until another string of the gloop shot out and tied around his wrist. He screamed and panted, then something clicked and he made his hand into a fist and commanded a prompt to use the flamethrower. It worked beautifully, the gloop receded but there was one issue that he overlooked. His suit was fireproof, that wasn't the problem but his flamethrower was damaged and it buffered. Soon the flame went off and the gloop pulled him closer to the ground. The mysterious liquid opened up and shaped itself like a bowl, ready to swallow Henry. The bowl gradually was turning into a ball slowly encapsulating Henry inside. The savior arrived. Neil threw a modern version of the Molotov inside and the gloop just chucked Henry's body outside. The gloop screeched and it was the foulest noise to enter Neil's and Henry's ears.

"Thanks, Neil"

"Run!"

They blasted off in the air and reached Josh who walked like a zombie.

"Josh let's go," said Neil hurriedly, "This place is biting to eat our asses."

"Money...so much money...I can use that, and that girl over there she is calling me" mumbled Josh.

"Carry him!" said Neil.

Neil and Henry tried to grab and pick up Josh using their jetpacks but he refused. He punched, scratched, and even used his flamethrower against them.

"Woah, Woah," said Henry backing off, "He is too far gone."

They watched Josh take a few steps before the gloop creeped up his body, broke the glass on his helmet and entered his nose and eyes. His body shivered, it spasmed, and out of his helmet came out all his organs. His brain, kidneys, liver, intestine, and heart which was still beating. Both gasped, their jaws dropped and their feet numb. They both looked at each other and without wasting a moment they flew off. The gloop shot up to catch Neil and Henry but they dodged the trajectory and boosted toward the portal.

"There, I see it!"

The gloop reflected the cosmic blue particles of the portal, looking like something straight out of the wizarding world. The gloop's final attempt to stop them from leaving was to shape itself as a wall between them and the portal. They both used their flamethrowers at the same time making a firewall in front of them, which breached the gloop wall and they flew through the portal and crashed into the airlock.

Each crewmate panting and gasping for air removes their helmets. Li was vomiting in a corner, and Jonsey sitting with a blank face, grilled.

Neil standing up and stretching his back said, " Are you guys okay?"

"Barely..." replied Henry softly "Where are the others?"

"Dead..." Jonsey sat back looking like an old man with paralysis, "The gloop...it swallowed them...it crept into their suits and just took them."

"That's it!" Henry got up on his feet and thundered, "Samantha! Don't you see? You are playing with life here!"

A screen dropped down from the ceiling and it displayed Samantha fixing her hair and pushing the glasses up her nose.

"As I said before, I am aware of the situation. I advise you to stick to the plan and explore the remaining two worlds. Else..."

"Else what!? Kill us? Do it then!" screamed Neil before he sat down pressing the palm of his hand against his forehead.

Henry looked over at Neil, a montage of Ronald's screams playing before his eyes. Henry gulped his saliva, clutched his helmet, and turned towards the screen.

"Samantha please," he said softly, "These worlds, realms, universes, whatever they are...they are not safe. How was this even a potential world? It was full of that 'gloop' It killed our men. How did that get past your tests?"

"I am not here to answer your questions, Mr. Henry. Do your job and save us from them," replied Samantha matching his tone.

Henry's eyes tore up "They are not so bad, are they? Yes, they ravage our food supplies and do terrible things sometimes but they are desperate. Their whole country fell, they were stripped from their homes and-"

"I am no talking about them...Mr. Henry" Samantha interrupted him

Henry and Samantha held intensely long eye contact. Henry tried to comprehend her words and Samantha's eyes radiating fear.

"I understand, you are feeling some strong emotions right now. But I assure you, if we are successful you would be heroes" Samantha continued.

Neil stood up once more and said, "I am not going in again, just kill me."

"Neil no!" Henry grabbed his shoulders

"I feared this moment would come," Samantha said confidently, "Care to look at the screen, Mr. Neil?"

Neil slowly picked his head up to gaze at the screen which displayed CCTV footage of his bedroom where his wife and a year-old daughter slept.

"What!" Neil's eyes widened and his body panicked, "Amanda! And my baby Joyce! Is this live?"

A laser then appeared on the peacefully sleeping baby.

"Wouldn't it be a shame if the mother woke up and saw her child scorched?" said Samantha calmly.

"Fine! I'll do it!" Neil fell on his knees, "I will do it..."

"Brilliant!" Samantha kept a straight face, "You would need new helmets, the rest of the suit is fine."

A drawer appeared on the right side of the airlock containing extra helmets. The four of them got their new helmets and got into position for the next portal.

"A-1074 appearing now" chimed an automated voice.

The four men stood still waiting for the portal to appear. Everyone stood there without hope but with a tremendous amount of fear. Blue particles once again thundered in mid-air, they collided, converged, and finally expanded forming another portal.

Henry looked at Neil, a face without his signature flair, a face without hope. Henry gulped and said, "We go in with hope; hope, of getting back here and back to our families. Let's go."

The four men stepped into the portal one after the other and found themselves in a lush and vibrant landscape with flora and fauna unknown to humans. The creatures were small but abundant and they seemed to be terrified of the invaders. They looked beautiful, with their hard red shells and their tiny feet. They were no bigger than the tip of their thumbs. Henry Gawked up above to the 'sky' and was baffled to observe what looked like water, suspended in mid-air. There were snake-like creatures, transparent and their heads were white cubes. The plants were strings, red and yellow, thick enough to swing from like 'Tarzan', the bark of the trees was pastel blue, with brown strings for leaves. The ground was gray with patches of liquid chrome. From which the red-shelled bugs emerged drenched in chrome.

"This is fascinating" uttered Li "This is the most beautiful place I have ever seen."

"Finally a peaceful place" continued Jonsey, "Why didn't they send us here first? The deaths would have been prevented."

"This place is as foul as the ones before..." Neil said walking with his dangling arms and a hopeless face, "Let's just get some samples and get out of here."

Henry agreed and the four men continued to walk into dense vegetation.

"Get the bark of that tree, that puddle of chrome over there, a few stings from that tree and dig the ground over that patch of gray", Henry ordered.

The men followed his order and began to extract samples. Henry crouched down to examine a mark on the ground. "What's this?" he whispered to himself "Oh no."

Henry turned to spot his fellow crewmates and he found Li with a small shovel in his hands. He was staring at something, standing straight, lifeless, like a statue. Henry hurriedly got himself near him, grabbed his shoulder, and shook him. Henry's face shrunk, he saw Li's eyes bleeding, and his pupils were scarlet red.

"Li! Snap out of it."

Li raised his arm pointing at a dark figure in the distance. Henry gradually turned to see. Time slowed down for him as his vision was tracing the landscape he heard a low-pitched noise. The noise elevated as his eyes were about to meet the dark figure. From his peripherals, he could see it, but he stopped. "If you see a dark humanoid figure in the distance, DO NOT look at it" Samantha's voice echoed in his head. Henry looked back at Li whose face spasmed, it looked like it was glitching like in a video game. The movements of his facial muscles were bizarre and inhumane. Henry felt the dark figure standing right behind him and he saw Li still gazing at it. Every pore on his face began to bleed, his body levitated out of Henry's grasp. The Dark figure pushed Henry and pierced Li's body. Henry ran for his life screaming, "Neil! Jonsey!" He approached the portal but right before he reached he tripped and fell face first, breaking the glass of his helmet and a shard impaling his forehead. He tried to ignore his pain but it was too much for him to bear. He got up limping, realizing that his leg was injured too. "Jonsey...Neil?"

Jonsey and Neil appeared before him.

"Come on Henry," Neil said.

Jonsey just stood there looking at his hands. He kept switching between the palm and the back of his hand. Neil picked Henry up and placed his arm around his shoulder.

"I have decided" uttered Jonsey with a different almost demonic voice, "I want to kill myself."

He removed his gloves to reveal sharp and long nails. He stabbed his face with every finger penetrating some part of his skin and vigorously scratched off the tissues.

"He is gone too..." Neil whispered and threw Henry into the portal before jumping in himself.

The portal closed and a team of doctors entered the airlock. They cleaned Henry's wound, sprayed a fast healing spray, and bandaged it. All of it was done in four minutes and Henry just sat there dumbfounded. The screen once again descended from the ceiling and on it was Samantha. "Well done boys! Just one more to go. This is the one, it has to be! Mark my word if this is not it, then I will have you two executed, I would have no use for you, plus it would be a terrible lawsuit."

"Get to the position lad..." Neil demanded.

Two almost lifeless bodies stood in their positions again waiting for the final portal to open.

"What did you find in there Henry?" asked Neil

"What do you mean?"

"I found this pretty fruit in there."

Neil took out a black glossy fruit partially covered with chrome, from his suit pocket, immediately removed his helmet, and took a bite.

"Neil No!"

Neil's body collapsed on the ground as if he had a heart attack. Henry, crying, snatched the fruit away from his hands but it was too late. Neil was already dying.

"I choose to die on my own terms" whimpered Neil, "I am sure I won't be coming out of this one...alive."

"You could have taken a shot Neil!" cried Henry, "Why?"

"Tell my wife and my little daughter...my Joyce... my baby... that dad loves her very mu..."

Neil's eyes were wide open but the soul had left him. A buzzer rang, the lights turned red and a team dragged Neil's dead body out of the airlock.

Henry didn't move. For the final time, blue particles collided, sparked, and expanded into another portal.

"A-3999 is now open," said an automated recorded voice.

Henry took a deep breath before crawling his way into the portal. He stood up once he was inside. It was a tunnel and at the very end of it was a single 'Black dot'. The greatest anomaly of them all. The infamous 'Black dot' he was said to stay away from. Henry sighed. "We are defeated, even though this is not eligible for them…" Henry turned back to enter the portal. He halted and contemplated for a few seconds before turning around. His legs drew towards the 'Black dot' and he sprinted. Without regret in his mind, he ran to the 'Black dot' and soon was engulfed by the darkness that came with it.

"HUH!", woke Fredrick with a jerk. He was in a glass capsule. He removed wires and other pipes attached to his body and after pressing some buttons got out of the capsule. His legs barely supported him. He stumbled his way out of the room and discovered hundreds if not thousands of the same glass capsules.

Fredrick was half-naked and thoroughly confused until he was greeted by a man in a suit and another man in a lab coat.

"Mr. Fredrick", said the man in the lab coat. "I see you are out of your capsule."

"What? Who is Fredrick?"

The man in the suit whispered to the lab coat, "It has happened again."

The man in the lab coat looked at Fredrick and said, "Or should I call you, Mr. Henry? You are going through 'Simulation Amnesia.' Come. I will help you remember.

Henry fell back hearing the situation and softly spoke, "It was all just-"

~A Simulation

Folklore
(This serves as an epilogue for each story)

Firefall

Fire now rains;

Believe me,

It even flows through the same drains;

The Ocean, which once was the great main,

Currently burns with what we call Hell's Flame.

Glory of the Same Summer Sun

The blazing ball was never seen;

A warm blanket, ever so serene.

Emitting light, Oh so bright!

The evil within still puts up a fight!

Saudade

The Children gathered around Richy's chair listening attentively

Richy: The beauty of those eyes are beyond any words I can utter. In my broken words, they were as mystical as the cosmos, as dense as the amazons, as mysterious as a Sherlock case, as bright as the sun, as calm as a Koala, as wild as the ocean, as comforting as a lover. I was lost in them. And the best part, they only saw me.

Cavern of the Lost Souls

Saved from a potential world-ending Nazi Invasion!

10th July 2060,

Researchers buckled up and ventured into "The Cavern of Lost Souls yet again. A pessimist would assume that they, like others before, won't return, but it was the day for believers. The intel that has been leaked as of now reads that Nazis resided in the cavern for decades all thanks to a scarce and advanced material that comes from a meteor. As far as our prediction goes, we think the material kept Hitler alive but he was ultimately killed by the soldiers that went in before. If that's the case, our chest has never been higher.

Astral Home

Owner of the simulation lab on TV: The thing is...there is no planet we can ever call our home again...it would just take too much brain power. Our ancestors decimated 'Earth' two thousand years ago.Plus what's not broken shouldn't be fixed. Hence it's a good idea to stay in these vast ships floating in an unknown but safe part of space. But people...their curiosities cannot be tamed, the precise reason why I founded this lab. To give people an entire lifetime on a fictitious earth. Live a life! A full life! Then come right back to your old one.

An interviewer: I understand, it's a beautiful concept that you have created Mr. Sofna. But tell me and honestly relieve my mind...are there any risks of totally forgetting your life? Is it possible to be that immersed in this artificial world?

Mr: Sofna: To my knowledge, absolutely not. They might suffer from what we call, 'Simulation amnesia' but not extending for more than a few hours.

Interviewer: Thank you so much Mr. Sofna for your time and we wish you all the best.

The TV was switched off.

Caretaker: Come on Henry, no more TV for you, get back to your room and catch some sleep.

Henry: Yes...thank you. He leaves

Caretaker 2: Poor soul. Been a year, still no memory

Caretaker 1: I know, there are hundreds like him.

She placed a dairy on the counter before switching off the lights of the room. Imprinted on the dairy's cover: "Trinity Hospital for the Mentally Ill"

Telos.

Author's Note

As of writing this passage about myself I am in third year of my English degree. My love for reading began during the great lockdown period when I randomly woke up at three o'clock at night and ordered a copy of Wuthering Heights. My bookshelf has grown significantly over the years and there is no stopping it. Storytelling is something that has always came to me naturally, from crafting an exaggerated tale of how I had to slay a beast to get a packet of salt from the grocery store to acting dramatically to finger guns. All that drama, spectacle, excitement, imagination, fantasy, comedy and so much more, defines who I am. Yes, I have been heavily influenced by films, and my love for them cannot be measured, it's just too much.

Anyway, I have said enough. I'll leave you with a quote from one of my favorite books.

"Droll thing life is -- that mysterious arrangement of merciless logic for a futile purpose. The most you can hope from it is some knowledge of yourself -- that comes too late -- a crop of inextinguishable regrets."

~Joseph Conrad's 'Heart of Darkness.'